A FOOLISH VOYAGE

Self-Discovery At Sea

NEIL HAWKESFORD

Published by

Copyright enquiries should be directed by e-mail to *neil@neilhawkesford.com*

ISBN-10: 1522768149

ISBN-13: 978-1522768142

To Mom & Dad for living with my foolishness all these years.
To Gail for sharing in it.
To 'Mor Gwas' for starting it.

Contents

Free Book Offer

As a thank you for buying my book I'd like to send you a gift.

It's a small collection of anecdotes about my time in the Royal Navy.

Just visit: https://www.neilhawkesford.com and you can download it completely free.

I hope you enjoy it.

Preface

This is the story of my adventures aboard 'Mor Gwas,' the little boat that was my home for a couple of years a long time ago.

It's the story of how I came to own her. The good times I had aboard her. And how I lost her after trying to sail across the Bay of Biscay single-handed.

It's been hard writing this stuff down. The events I describe affected me deeply. It wasn't until I started writing that I realised how deeply. I found that time had numbed my feelings. But the pain and the pleasure were still there, raw as when I first experienced them. There were tears when some of these things happened. There were tears when I wrote about them thirty years later. Maya Angelou once said:

"There is no greater agony than bearing an untold story inside you"

Indeed.

Preface

I've chosen to call my book 'A Foolish Voyage' because many will think it was. I'll admit to being foolish, I was then and I am now. But I'm a fan of foolishness. Many great people have praised foolishness.

The Greek philosopher Epictetus said:

"If you want to improve, be content to be thought foolish and stupid"

And of course, Steve Jobs said:

"Stay young, stay foolish"

As the Greek playwright Sophocles said:

"And if to some my tale seems foolishness I am content that such could count me fool"

1

End Of The Road

I FOUND the harness quick release by feel as the clouds of choking red dust made it impossible to see. The car had come to rest upside down in a ditch after barrel rolling three or four times. My helmet was hard up against the roof as I dropped my legs onto the underside of the dashboard and twisted myself out through the smashed side window.

I crawled out of the wreckage, calling out for my navigator as I did so. "Dave, Dave are you OK? Dave". He shouted back, "Yeah I'm here, I'm fine, are you getting out or what?". Dave, it seemed, had wasted no time in exiting the car and was standing up on the bank a few yards away.

I clambered up to join him and sat down on the soft dusty grass. As he took off his helmet Dave started laughing. "I told you that bend tightened, but you kept it planted didn't you?" He was right, I'd long since realised that once committed to a bend there was rarely any point in lifting or braking and hell, we'd nearly got away with it. But the rear wheels had dropped into an ever deepening ditch. We were travelling sideways at about 50mph. There was only ever going to be one outcome.

I looked down at the underside of my faithful MkII Ford

1

Escort, it looked like the floor pan was the only straight panel left on the car. We'd had a biggy that's for sure and I was grateful that Dave and I had escaped uninjured, but I was hurting none the less. I knew this was it, we really were at the end of the road.

I was broke and there was no way I could afford to get the car repaired. This time, there was no coming back. I'd lived and breathed rallying for years, it was going to leave a big hole in my life. As I sat and watched the other cars pass by I wondered how on earth I was going to fill it.

2

Dropping Out
_____

THE FOLLOWING MONDAY morning saw me cycling to work as usual. I had a job as Warranty Clerk in a local garage, but as I pedalled into town it struck me that my reason for working there was written off same as my car. I'd only taken the job because of my rallying. It was a bike ride away which meant it didn't matter if the car was in bits at home (it usually was between events). Not only that but it gave me access to tools and spares at trade prices, and, of course, it paid the bills.

That said it was mind-numbingly boring and now I began to wonder why I should carry on doing it. The job had been no fun for a while anyway as there'd been rumours of redundancies and closure flying about the place for months. Everyone I worked with was pissed off and the atmosphere was generally tense and unhappy.

To be honest, I'd been as worried as everyone else because losing my job would have endangered my rallying, now it didn't seem to matter. Maybe that's what led to the events that followed a few weeks later.

One morning at tea-break, the guys we were all sitting around gassing about the latest rumours. Derek Allen the workshop manager came into the canteen for a brew. As usual, he was bombarded with questions. He just shrugged his shoulders and gave his by now monotonous impression of 'Manuel' from Fawlty Towers saying "I know nothing". By then I'd reached a point where I just didn't care. I'd had enough of all this nonsense and without a thought, I stood up and said, "This is f!!!g ridiculous, I'm going to see Barfield and ask him what the f!!ks going on".

Barfield was the recently appointed General Manager. Most of us believed he'd been put in place as the 'hatchet man'. As I walked out of the canteen Derek shook his head "Oh no Neil don't, leave things lie, we'll know soon enough". I ignored him.

Barfield's office sat just off the main new car showroom and was surrounded by glass, so I could see he was at his desk. I knocked on the door and walked in. He knew who I was as my job required me to work with the sales staff in the showroom but if he knew my name he didn't use it. "Yes, what do you want," he said dropping his pen on the desk. I kept things simple. I told him that all these rumours of redundancy were causing real pain to folks on the shop floor and that work was suffering. I asked if there was anything he could tell us that would help clear the air.

While I was talking, I could see that he was getting redder and redder in the face, until suddenly, he launched himself out of his leather chair. He drew himself up to his full 5'5' and screamed at me. "Redundancy! Redundancy! If you're so f!!!g interested in redundancy you can be the first one to go. You're redundant, get your stuff and get off the premises now!"

Over his shoulder, I could see out to the showroom where Liz, one of the Sales girls, was standing with a middle-aged couple. She'd been using all her charms to try and sell them a new Mini Metro. Now she'd stopped talking and all three of them were staring with their mouths wide open. Mr Barfield's words had reached their ears too. Shocked as I was I've long had the somewhat rare talent of being able to remain calm when all those around me have lost it, and so it was now. I calmly replied, "I'm sorry Mr Barfield, but you can't make me redundant just like that",

4

his response was even more maniacal. "Yes, yes I can, I can do anything I like, I'm the f!!!g General Manager!"

Now perhaps I should have taken this a bit more seriously. Maybe my recent high-speed motorsport accident gave me a different perspective on things. But I couldn't help but find the whole thing amusing. The workshop managers recent 'Manuel' impression had brought to mind Fawlty Towers. Now it seemed that Mr Barfield was intent on doing a Basil Fawlty loses it impression. I held back from laughing, but I guess my quizzical smile didn't help his mood any. As I turned to leave his office he came round from behind his desk and followed me out, still ranting. "Get back to your office, get your coat, get off the premises, you're redundant as of now".

As I walked back towards the workshop he stormed ahead of me. By the time I reached my office door all the workshop lads had downed tools and were staring in amazement. He yelled at Derek Allen demanding that I cleared my desk immediately. He wanted me escorted off the premises within the next 10 minutes. With that he marched back to the showroom.

Everyone crowded around me desperate to know what the hell I'd done to provoke him so much. As I stuffed the few things I wanted into my rucksack I told them, "Well, you've got a lunatic in charge lads, good luck with that, I'm out of here". Then I jumped on my bike and peddled off, never to return.

I had a clear conscience, I'd been polite, I'd been honest, I'd acted with the best intentions. There was no way he could label my dismissal as redundancy, he'd lost it and gone too far, I wasn't going to let that go. During the following week I took some advice and started a claim for unfair dismissal. Six months later, I found myself at an Industrial Tribunal facing two barristers representing the Company.

Against all advice, I chose not to have a Solicitor and defended myself. No one knew what had happened better than me. I just told the truth. That simple tactic made it impossible for the smart arsed legals to knock me off track, and to cut a long day short I won. I came out with a compensation payout which, although small in today's terms, was, at the time, more money than I'd ever had in my grubby little mitts before.

Over the following weeks as the dust settled I started thinking about my options. The whole episode had left me feeling disillusioned. Up until then I'd believed that once you had a job it was safe as long as you worked hard and kept your nose clean. Now I knew different. Although I'd won the case and justice had done the reality was that I'd taken an employer to a tribunal and it was a black mark on my CV. Future employers might consider me a troublemaker, why would they take the risk? So it looked like getting another job would be hard, and, to be honest, I wasn't even sure I wanted one.

Without the rallying to add spice to my life everything now seemed a bit empty and boring. But hey, I was young free and single and with some money in the bank. After what had happened my self-confidence was high and I had a strong urge to do something completely different. The slate had been wiped clean and I was ready for a new challenge.

3

Call Of The Sea

IN THE SIX months I'd spent waiting for the Tribunal I'd had plenty of time to re-evaluate my life and to consider my options. Since leaving school I'd spent three years in the Royal Navy and two more working in South Africa. Yet here I was at the age of 26 back living with my parents. I wasn't in a relationship. My small circle of friends were either from rallying or my old job and I was already losing touch with them. Now I was jobless.

I was starting to think that somehow I just wasn't cut out to do what everybody else was doing. I was starting to think that maybe I should take a completely new direction. I'd found my mind turned more and more to the sea and sailing.

I'd sailed dinghies in the Navy. I'd always felt at home on the water, and the more I read the more I found myself being drawn to the thought that I should move to the coast or even buy a boat. I was reading a lot about boats and sailing but of all the books I read there was one in particular that I couldn't stop thinking about. That book was 'Shrimpy' by Shane Acton.

Long since out of print, it's the story of how a guy sailed an 18ft plywood Caprice daysailer around the world. Reading it opened my eyes to the possibility that there was an incredible escape open to me. It showed me that I could experience adventure and freedom in a way I'd never have thought possible. I started buying sailing magazines and reading more and more about single-handed sailing. I scouring the small ads looking at similar boats to Shane's Caprice. And so it was that I saw an 18ft Hurley Silhouette for sale on the South Coast at a good price.

Also a Robert Tucker design, the Silhouette represented the next generation on from the Caprice and I had the money to buy her. There wasn't a shadow of doubt in my mind. This was exactly what I needed in my life right now. If Shane Acton could do it then so could I. Not only would I have a place of my own but I'd have a vehicle to travel the world.

I know that it may seem ridiculous to many that I could consider an 18ft boat to be a viable long-term home but remember I was young and prepared to try anything. I was long overdue leaving home and I'd now seen plenty of evidence that it was possible to live comfortably without bricks and mortar walls. There was another factor at play as well. The rebel in me, the one that always wanted to do things that most others wouldn't consider, the rebel egged me on.

Many years before I'd dreamed of owning a motorhome and driving around the coast of the UK, living in the van and perhaps drawing and painting for a living. I know nothing about my ancestry, but I wouldn't be at all surprised to find that there is some gypsy blood in my lineage somewhere. As my life progressed I tried to put down roots quite a few times and for one reason or another it never worked. It's a strange paradox that I like my own space, I like the idea of 'home' and yet I've never found one place that feels right to stay for any length of time. I guess that's why a caravan or a boat suits me, because when I tire of the view out of the windows I can change it.

My theory would seem to hold true as I'm now once again aboard a boat living life as a sea gypsy.

Anyway back to my story, the same day I saw the ad I rang the seller and arranged to go and look at the boat. I don't recall the details but it doesn't matter, I saw her, I fell in love with her and I bought her.

I decided to name her 'Mor Gwas' which in the old Cornish language means 'Sea Servant'.

I was now a boat owner.

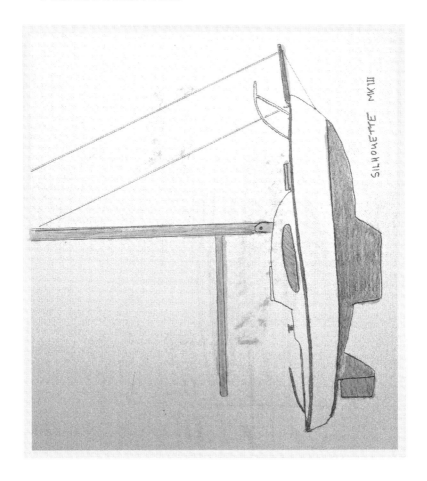

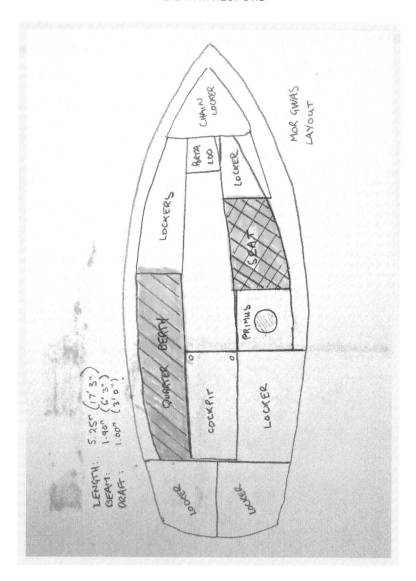

4

The Boatyard

IF YOU'RE familiar with a Hurley Silhouette you'll know they're small. Less than eighteen feet from stem to stern, a cabin just large enough for a single bunk, a few lockers and sitting headroom.

The idea of living in such a small space may seem absurd. But as I was to prove, it's not only possible but perfectly comfortable.

So here I was, about to spend my first night aboard my own boat. It felt good, even if she was only sitting on a trailer in a boatyard. I had some work to do before 'Mor Gwas' could go in the water though and I was looking forward to getting started.

I slept like a log. In the morning and wolfed down a hearty breakfast. Egg, sausage, bacon and fried bread washed down with grapefruit juice and tea. Already I was proving that there was no need to starve just because a Primus stove was my only means of cooking.

Over the next few days I painting inside the cabin. Sanded and varnished woodwork and applying a fresh coat of antifouling paint. I discovered how noxious anti-foul is when I developed a rash on my hands and face and a nose running like a tap. A lesson learned.

The following weeks were a test. The weather was lousy. Strong

Northerly winds that gusted up to 65 mph at times, torrential rain and bitter cold.

My Primus stove packed up and I had to buy a new one.

'Mor Gwas's' trailer became an island surrounded by mud and water.

The cabin was permanently damp and cold and frankly, things got a bit miserable.

I threw myself into the work, inside the cabin when the weather was particularly bad, outside when I could.

I often cycled around Gosport and Lee-on-Solent to get supplies and started to feel at home. To be fair, I wasn't a complete stranger to the place. During my time in the Royal Navy I'd been stationed at HMS Daedalus just down the road.

On one of my trips into town the rain started coming down so I was pedalling hard to get back to the boat. I came round a corner to find a red traffic light shining in my face. The traffic lights were there only because there was a raised manhole with a barrier around it. I could clearly see that there was nothing coming the other way so I ignored the light and carried on. It must have been a good mile further on that I pulled over to the side of the road to tighten the straps of my rucksack.

Suddenly a policeman on a pushbike stopped right alongside me. His red face and heaving chest indicated that he'd been peddling his old upright hard. As he removed his helmet and gulped air he gasped "Didn't you hear me shouting? Why didn't you stop".

I apologised and said that I'd not heard him, and that if I'd been trying to outrun him I'd hardly have stopped at the curb like I had. He then got out his notebook and said he'd seen me ignore a red traffic light and did I understand that I'd committed a traffic offence? Once again my calm nature and sense of humour did me no favour. I apologised again but he seemed intent on getting the maximum benefit from his exertions.

As he regained his breath he asked where I lived and when I answered "on a boat up the road", he seemed deflated. "No permanent address then". "No" I answered. At that he started putting his notebook away and said: "Well don't let me catch you jumping red lights again". Then he pedalled off.

He left me bemused, wondering if I was now truly a gypsy living outside the law.

Over the next few days the weather improved, my jobs list got smaller and I even 'moved 'house'.

When I'd arrived at the yard 'Mor Gwas' had been sitting towards the back of the place surrounded by other boats. But as the yard came alive and pre-season work commenced these boats had to be moved around.

As 'Mor Gwas' was scheduled to be launched within the week I was moved out by the quay. I even got a sea view (well actually a Portsmouth Harbour view but nice all the same). After two weeks living aboard a landlocked boat the big day finally arrived. 'Mor Gwas' was due to be craned in on the morning tide. but problems with the crane meant that it was mid-afternoon before she was lifted and put down on the now dry slipway.

It was one in the morning before the returning tide lapped at her stern and shortly after she was afloat!

It was only a short hop under engine from the slip round to my pontoon berth. To be honest, I was grateful there was no one around to watch me manoeuvre with the outboard for the first time. All went well though and once I'd tied up I had a good look at the bilges and hull fittings to check she was watertight. I needn't have worried. Everything was dry as a bone.

By 2 am I was in my bunk trying to adjust to the sounds of squeaking fenders, creaking mooring lines and the gentle rocking of a boat afloat. It all seemed strange to me then but before long they would be the most comforting and natural sensations in the world.

After a few days getting used to being afloat I was keen to get sailing. So at the beginning of April I untied 'Mor Gwas' from the pontoon and motored out into the harbour for the first time.

After my years of dinghy sailing it took a while to get out of the habit of leaning out over the windward side every time the boat heeled. I suppose the fact that 'Mor Gwas' was only slightly longer than some of the dinghies I'd sailed didn't help any.

But once I'd gained confidence that the boat could heel without danger of capsize I started to enjoy things. The winds were light in any case and I started putting into practice all the things I'd been reading about for so long.

Pointing: i.e. sailing the boat into the wind, reaching: i.e. sailing across the wind, and running: i.e. sailing with the wind.

'Mor Gwas' proved easy to handle, she needed only a light touch on the tiller and it was great to feel her moving through the water after all the weeks ashore.

I slept well that night. It'd been 3 months since I bought her and I'd been at Quay Lane for close on a month, I was happy 'Mor Gwas' was seaworthy. I knew she sailed well and that I knew enough to handle her. It was time to start the adventure proper.

My goal was never in doubt, I was aiming for Falmouth in Cornwall, a place I knew well and a place I'd always wanted to live. It would be a couple of hundred miles of coastal sailing, I'd learn as I went and visit places I'd never been. It would be our first proper voyage together

5

Portsmouth - Falmouth

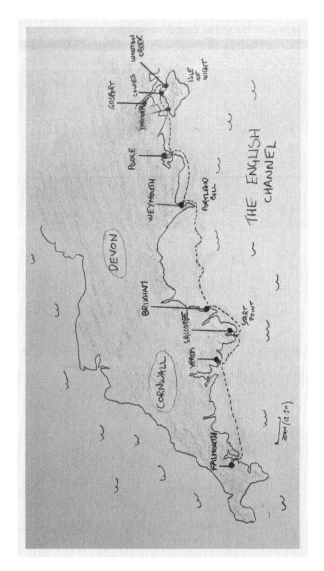

South Coast Voyage

SO IT WAS on a dull breezy day, 'Mor Gwas' and I left Quay Lane for the last time and headed down towards Portsmouth Harbour entrance.

I was nervous because Portsmouth is a busy port and I didn't want to get mixed up with the many large ships manoeuvring around. I was so cautious that when, as I approached the entrance proper, I saw a big grey vessel heading towards me. I did an 180' turn and headed back up the harbour to keep clear.

It turned out to be RFA 'Plumleaf' coming into dock. I waited nearly an hour before plucking up the courage to make a dash for the Solent.

Once out of the relative shelter of the harbour 'Mor Gwas' was soon bouncing her way through quite a heavy chop. I set course for Wooton Creek on the Isle of Wight. I hadn't exactly been ambitious with this first passage as Wooton Creek lies only a couple of miles across the Solent from Portsmouth. But hey, I'd be making landfall on an offshore island and that can't be bad for a first trip.

Apart from a jammed jib roller (something that was to cause me bigger problems later) the crossing was uneventful. And a short while later I was motoring into the creek.

As I meandered around looking for somewhere to moor, I was puzzled to see a line of big wooden piles equally spaced and driven into the middle of the creek. It was only the fact that there was already a boat moored between them that gave me a clue what to do.

It's simple really, you tie the bow to one pile and the stern to another and then adjust the lines so that the boat is sitting in the middle. I hadn't come across this before and it took me a while to sort out enough rope, get it wrapped around the piles and to get 'Mor Gwas' in the right place.

I was more than ready for a cuppa by the time I'd finished and I drank it with a warm glow of satisfaction at having completed our first 'voyage'.

Wooton Creek wasn't exactly the tranquil haven I'd anticipated.

Construction had begun on a new ferry terminal. And the following morning I was woken by a frightful low growling and rumbling sound that seemed to shake 'Mor Gwas' where she floated.

I stuck my head out of the hatch to see a huge tug called 'Kamsar' manoeuvring a massive barge close by. As I finished breakfast this barge started work driving huge steel piles into the mud, I didn't stay long after that.

A pleasant sail West up the Solent in light airs and warm sunshine brought me to my next port of call, Cowes.

Looking back I can't believe I even considered going there let alone staying in the marina. Cowes, of course, is THE place to be for the upper echelons of yachting. I decided against strolling up to the Royal Yacht Squadron clubhouse to see if I could get a shower.

'Mor Gwas' was tucked away amongst some similar sized boats at one end of a finger pontoon. I ignored the fact that these other boats were all tenders of one sort or another.

As I walked down the pontoon towards town I passed 'Marionette' one of the Whitbread round the world boats. There were also several Admirals Cup racing boats. And row upon row of high-tech yachts all perfectly kept and gleaming with huge stainless steel winches and fittings.

As I walked through the town with its posh chandleries, clothing shops and cafes I felt more than a little out of place. I clearly wasn't a proper yachtie.

It struck me though that most of the folks I could see were no more than 'hangers on'. Strolling around hoping that some of the 'round the world sailing' glamour might rub off on them. It seemed that a lot of the expensive boats down in the marina probably never went out of the Solent.

I smiled to myself, what would they think if they knew anything about the adventure I was on.

The following day I slipped out of Cowes on a foggy morning and headed down The Solent again towards Yarmouth. The sun broke through as I left and the day turned warm. I couldn't believe how many sails I could see on the water. It was only the arrival of the Lymington-Yarmouth ferry that seemed to clear a way through to the harbour entrance. I followed her in.

I was directed to a berth alongside an old motor cruiser. I soon found out she was home to Jack and Susan who took my lines and then invited me aboard for coffee. It was my first taste of real liveaboard hospitality.

I couldn't help but draw a comparison with Cowes where I'd spoken to no one. The following lunchtime I left on the ebb tide and pointed 'Mor Gwas' out through the Needles Channel towards the open sea for the first time.

The winds were light and with the tide pushing us along we were soon in clear water. I was pleased about that as the Needles Channel has a nasty reputation.

There are four main navigational hazards, Hurst Narrows, Shingles Bank, The Bridge and The Trap. The names tell you all you need to know.

It was a pleasant sail though and I even managed to get the home built wind vane self-steering working for a while. That was odd, standing in the companionway watching it pull the tiller back and forth as 'Mor Gwas' made her own way through the water.

The late departure and light winds meant that I had to make my approach into Poole in darkness. The Swatch Channel entrance is wide and well marked though so I had no trouble.

Poole Harbour is one of the largest natural harbours in the world. But much of the water is shallow and there are many channels marked with buoys and lights. I was heading for Town Quay quite a way in.

I was concentrating hard, standing in the cockpit, tiller between my legs, trying to read the chart in the light of my head torch. I was trying to identify the many static and flashing red, green and white lights ahead of me. At one point, I looked astern and had the fright of my life. It was the huge looming shape of a Cherbourg ferry steaming up behind me. A glowing bow wave rolling along in front of her.

I turned 'Mor Gwas' hard to starboard out of the main channel and a few minutes later she glided past, eerily quiet, leaving 'Mor Gwas' rolling in her wake.

I recovered my composure and picking up the channel again found my way to the quay. It was a bit of a challenge mooring up as the quay wall was uneven. My fenders kept falling into the gaps making them useless. I noticed that all the other boats alongside were using a plank of wood to bridge the gaps, but I hadn't got one.

Luckily some folks on another boat spotted my predicament and allowed me to tie alongside them.

I spent a day in Poole resting and sorting the boat out. Town Quay was busy with tourists and at low tide they'd stand on the quay above staring down into the boat pointing and making comments. I didn't mind, it wasn't so long ago I'd have been doing it myself.

On Wednesday 20th April, I left Poole heading for Weymouth.

This proved to be the most challenging leg of the entire trip, despite a forecast of 3 to 4 the wind increased to a good Force 5. The sea was choppy and for the first time I experienced some big swells. It was a roller coaster ride. I'll confess to being more than a little concerned that I'd pushed my luck too far.

But gradually I began to realise that 'Mor Gwas' was riding along quite nicely. Only the occasional sloppy wave dropped any water into the cockpit. The drains soon cleared it. It took me 10 hours to reach Weymouth. I spent the entire time in the cockpit hanging onto the tiller. I felt queasy and I didn't eat or drink, my navigation was rudimentary as I relied on the waterproof chart a few compass bearings and the MkI eyeball.

As I approached Weymouth the wind picked up again. And, when I pulled the furling line on the jib to roll it up it jammed. This left the sail flogging horrendously in the wind.

I couldn't sheet it in as the wind was too strong so I had to lash the tiller and crawl onto the foredeck to secure it. 'Mor Gwas' was pitching and rolling all over the place and despite the fact that I

A Foolish Voyage

was wearing my harness securely clipped onto the boat it was scary.

Eventually, I managed to get the sail under control and secure. I got the engine started and steered us into the sheltered and calm waters of Weymouth Harbour. I was cold, wet, exhausted and very grateful to be safely tied up alongside.

As it turned out I arrived in Weymouth just in time because for the next 5 days the weather turned unseasonably wet and windy. I listened to the forecast daily watching for a good weather window.

The next leg of the trip meant passing the biggest hurdle of the whole voyage... Portland Bill.

Portland Bill and its associated Tidal Race is without a doubt the most feared barrier to those sailing the South coast of England. The Bill sticks well out into the English Channel and creates huge South flowing tidal eddies either side of it. These tidal sets can run at 8-10 knots, and for 9 hours out of every 12 these eddies collide just South of the Bill over the shallow water of the Portland Ledge.

Even in calm weather the Race is full of steep standing waves and many a yacht has been caught out by the tide and sucked into the turmoil.

So far in the trip every time I'd mentioned that Falmouth was my destination the first thing I'd heard was a sharp intake of breath. That was usually followed by something like "you'll have to get round Portland Bill - that's a yacht killer that is". Of course, many of these folks had never been more than a few miles from their home port, but none the less they had a point.

I was well aware of the danger and had no intention of taking any risks particularly in a small, slow sailboat with only a low-powered outboard engine. To clear the Race to seaward, it's recommended to pass 3-5nm out. To do that from Weymouth also means heading East for a ways to clear the Shambles Bank from which the strong tide runs straight into the Race. In effect, this meant that I'd have to take a 15nm detour before I even got round the Bill and that would just be the start of a long trip across Lyme Bay.

21

This option held no appeal. So I planned to take the far shorter inshore passage hugging the shore (100-150m out) and trying to avoid the many submerged lobster pots.

I could only attempt this passage in calm conditions, good visibility and with perfect timing. There could be no ifs buts or maybes, I was entirely in the hands of the weather Gods.

I hadn't been to Weymouth before and so I had no trouble keeping myself occupied during the time I was there. Having made my entrance in pouring rain and lousy visibility I hadn't seen the huge sweeping seafront and beach. It came as quite a surprise when on the first day I walked away from the harbour and suddenly found myself on a traditional seaside promenade.

The prom and beach were sheltered from the Westerly wind and with the sun shining it seemed surreal. The beach was packed, there were people swimming and surfing, the amusement arcades were doing a booming trade, I even had an ice cream.

In the evening, I treated myself to a slap up meal. Grapefruit cocktail, steak and kidney pie with potatoes and veg, followed by apple pie and ice cream all washed down with a pint of lager and a coffee. Not only was it nice to eat sitting at a table after so long eating from my lap but the bill came to a whopping £3.65…… those were the days eh?

One problem with being moored so close to the town though was the temptation to spend money. The odd cuppa, a newspaper, a snack, it all added up, so whenever I could I'd get away with long walks around the coast.

One time I walked out to Nothe Fort which sits on a peninsula jutting Eastward from the harbour. The views over Weymouth Bay and Portland Harbour were spectacular.

Apart from walks I spent quite a bit of time working on 'Mor Gwas'. I'd now sailed her long enough to find things that needed improvement and, of course, there were other jobs that I'd not had time to finish at Quay Lane.

One of the improvements I made was to add reefing pennants to the eyelets in the mainsail. These are simply light pieces of rope permanently attached. They make it far easier to secure the bundled sail when it's reduced in size as the wind strength increases, I'd struggled with this a few times too many.

It was in Weymouth that I first witnessed what I've since discovered is a far from an unusual occurrence. Specifically the somewhat casual attitude some French yachtsman seem to have when it comes to mooring up.

I hasten to add that I'm not by any means wishing to tar all the mariners of that great sailing nation with the same brush. My ultimate sailing hero Bernard Moitessier was French and there are many others whose seamanship I can only aspire to. But at the other end of the scale there are some who are just plain crazy.

On this particular day a 36 ft Beneteau motored into the harbour. The two guys on board were dressed in jeans and leather jackets and had the obligatory Gauloises hanging from their mouths.

It looked to me as if they'd just stolen the boat and motored it from wherever they'd come from. The jib was tightly furled and the mainsail was still in its cover. I watched with amazement as they casually crunched the boat alongside the harbour wall without a single fender deployed. They jumped up on the quay, hastily wrapped a couple of lines around the bollards and then immediately strolled off towards town.

They'd arrived on the top of a Spring tide. In Weymouth that means the water is going to drop some 2.5m (8ft). When they'd still not reappeared a few hours later the boats mooring lines were so tight it looked as if she'd be left hanging off the quay in mid-air.

As I helped the harbour master adjust the lines and add some springs so she'd sit comfortably he told me he'd lost track of the number of times he'd had to do it. He reckoned they'd probably disappear without paying any harbour dues.

Sure enough when I got up the following morning they'd gone.

A week after I arrived the weather started to settle down. The forecast talked about Easterly 3-4 decreasing 3 and high pressure starting to build.

Boats started arriving saying what great sailing weather it was, one of them called 'Pepper' moored alongside 'Mor Gwas' and we got chatting. It turned out that the owner, Jed, came from my old home town of Lichfield and his crew, Bob, from just up the road in Rugeley.

As we talked I discovered that they were planning to leave for Brixham the following morning. When I said that I was doing the same Jed said "well when you get in you can moor alongside us on our swinging mooring. I'm pretty sure I can find you a free mooring to use for a few days after that".

If I needed any further encouragement that was it, tomorrow I'd face the dreaded Portland Bill.

At ten the following morning 'Pepper' and 'Mor Gwas' motored out into the bay and set sail. 'Pepper' immediately set off South East to go round the Shambles and clear The Race well offshore. Being a deep keeled performance cruiser she was fast and their plan made perfect sense. 'Mor Gwas' was a shallow draft bilge keeler and slow, so as I said, I'd opted to take the inshore passage.

As I sailed slowly past Portland though the wind started dying away. It was critical to keep the tide so I wasted no time in firing up the outboard. I'd put another fuel can aboard and given the engine a good service in anticipation of such an event.

After all the build up The Bill turned out to be a bit of an anti-climax. But for that I was grateful. I motored round close inshore in a flat calm, but looking to seaward I could still see the white crests of breaking water catching the sunlight.

I kept the motor running until I was well clear and switched it off, mightily pleased to have finally passed the dreaded Bill. I had a limited fuel reserve and had already motored for a couple of hours. I knew that to leave enough to enter Brixham I'd have to rely on the sails for the trip across Lyme Bay. Whatever the wind.

With it being light and variable, I knew it was going to be slow going. And as I hauled up the main and unfurled the jib I wondered how 'Pepper' was doing. For the rest of the day I alternated between helming and using the self-steering. The slight conditions meant I had no trouble making drinks and something to eat. By mid-afternoon, for the first time, I had a 360' horizon with no sign of land, and then it went completely calm.

The only sounds were water lapping the hull and the gentle creaking of rope. It was surreal, the sun was hot and I felt as if I was thousands of miles away on some tropical ocean.

I knew that this was also going to be my first all night passage and as darkness fell my senses came alive. There was a decent moon but now and again cloud would roll by and it became pitch black.

I wasn't using any navigation lights as my battery wouldn't run them all night. So I was keeping a good lookout and using them only if I saw any other lights. I also had a big torch ready in the cockpit.

As it turned out I only saw two other vessels all night, the first one scared me. It never got close enough for me to identify, but it was sizeable and moving fast. From what I could see she was on a collision course, I could see my masthead lights were on and I shone the torch into my sail to try and make 'Mor Gwas' more visible. Eventually I chickened out, fired up the outboard and motored well out of the way. I may not have been in any real danger but better safe than sorry. I now know better with regard to the big torch though. Don't waste time shining it in your sails, shine it straight at the thing coming towards you!

The second vessel was a small fishing boat. She did what I mentioned above and shone a big spotlight straight at me, she wasn't worried about collision she was just curious. With my night vision ruined I just held up my hand in greeting and she turned away.

As dawn broke I could see land ahead and managed to identify some landmarks. Checking the chart, I discovered that we'd been set a little North during the night. We were on the Northern side of Torbay heading for Torquay rather than Brixham.

The wind had picked up a bit and, of course, the new heading put it right on the nose, I checked the fuel and decided I'd got enough to motor the rest of the way. So at 5.30am I puttered into the sheltered crystal clear water of Brixham harbour and soon spotted 'Pepper' sitting happily on a mooring.

There was an empty buoy close by so I picked that up rather than disturb them. It'd taken 20 hours to get here, I'd not slept at all, it didn't take long to nod off.

I only slept for about 4 hours though before I heard knocking on the hull. It was Jed and Bob from 'Pepper' coming over to say hi, they'd arrived in the early evening and turned in slightly concerned I'd not arrived. They were on their way ashore for a mooch about, so I got changed quickly and grabbed a lift.

Once ashore we split up and I went in search of a full English breakfast and a mug of tea, it went down extremely well I can tell you.

Afterwards, I walked about for a bit soaking in the atmosphere. The inner harbour and quay were buzzing with activity. I found a replica of Francis Drake's ship the 'Golden Hind' moored alongside. Apparently she had a crew of 60 but I was staggered how small she seemed. As lunchtime approached I met up with the lads again and we dropped into one of the waterside pubs for a few pints which was nice. But the beer, the sun and my lack of sleep were starting to have an adverse effect on me so we soon headed back to the boats.

Next day saw the weather turning again and I spent the day aboard catching up on sleep and generally relaxing. 'Mor Gwas' was moored quite near the lifeboat station and later that evening I was startled by a loud bang that rattled 'Mor Gwas' from stem to stern.

It didn't take me long to realise that it was one of the maroons fired off to summon the lifeboat crew. I watched as two more maroons were fired and then saw car headlights sweeping down the road towards the station. Within a few minutes, the kitted out crew were in a fast tender and climbing aboard the moored lifeboat. Engines were fired up, on came navigation lights, searchlights and the blue flashing light and soon she was powering out to sea.

The work these guys do is incredible and on another mooring close by there was a clear reminder of the dangers they face. It was the brand new Penlee lifeboat. It was on an overnight stop before carrying on its journey to replace the temporary boat which in turn had replaced the 'Solomon Browne'. 'Solomon Browne' had been lost some 18 months earlier. She'd been trying to rescue the crew of the coaster 'Union Star' after she suffered engine failure in 90-knot winds. and was pushed into the cliffs near the Tater Du lighthouse not far from Penzance. Sixteen people lost their lives that night including all eight of the lifeboat crew.

The next few days were spent similarly to those I spent weather-bound in Weymouth. I walked the coastal path out to Berry Head and explored in and around Brixham.

Between times I carried on with the seemingly never ending jobs list aboard 'Mor Gwas'. Soon enough though the weather cleared up and I was able to say goodbye to Jed and Bob and set sail for my next stop, Salcombe.

I had a hard 10-hour beat to get there but by now I was getting the hang of this sailing lark and I pushed 'Mor Gwas' and myself harder than I'd ever done. Exciting though it is to be ploughing along with the lee rail well under water it's not the most efficient way of sailing a little bilge keeled boat. So I reefed down and found I made better progress.

The breeze was stiff and pretty much on the nose so I had to tack back and forth. Visibility was good though which made my navigation easier. I was pleased to find that I had calculated the tidal streams correctly. That made my passing of Start Point relatively straightforward. An hour or so later I was rounding Prawle Point heading into Salcombe.

Once again I was seeing somewhere I'd not been before and despite the rain it was a spectacular approach. The entrance is quite narrow and guarded by a sand bar that can be extremely dangerous in stiff onshore winds or large swells. In 1916, the lifeboat 'William and Emma' was overwhelmed on the bar with the loss of 13 lives. On the day I arrived it was invisible.

Once over the bar you are in a steep sided valley and seemingly sailing straight for the trees. But then the river turns hard right and you can see the town and river. The estuary is actually a flooded valley in some ways like the famous Rias of Northern Spain, it's beautiful.

I was noticing a trend, it seemed the further West I sailed the more beautiful the coast became.

I tied up to a vacant visitors mooring and after something to eat slept well all night. The following day dawned sunny and warm. As I sat in the cockpit with my cup of tea I looked around in wonder at my new surroundings. The steep sides of the valley were heavily wooded, the towns multicoloured houses spread up the hill looking like the picture on a biscuit box.

On the opposite bank, there were little coves with sandy beaches, rocky cliffs and bright green vegetation. The water was crystal clear blue and green. This was quite a contrast to that grey muddy berth back at Quay Lane.

After breakfast I pumped up the dinghy and rowed ashore, I walked up through the town and out towards the harbour entrance. I found a spot high above the river facing out to sea looking over the Bar. There wasn't a breath of wind, the air was still, the clouds had come down low and settled on top of the hills behind me. The air was scented with wild flowers. I sat there for a long while taking it all in. It was magical and I smiled at the thought of what I and my little boat had done and wondered what other delights were still to come.

I stayed in Salcombe for a couple of days before leaving for the River Yealm some 15nm West. It was a sign of my growing confidence in 'Mor Gwas' and my own abilities that I set off with a forecast of S veering WNW force 4/ 5 locally 6.

Not only that but I sailed off the mooring and out of Salcombe without using the engine. The sea was as rough as I'd sailed in, with quite large breaking swells bearing down on the port quarter.

I kept thinking they were going to break over the stern and fill the cockpit, but 'Mor Gwas' just lifted like a cork as they passed harmlessly below.

There was plenty of spray flying over the bow though and I made a mental note to get a sprayhood and dodgers sorted out in Falmouth.

It was a short exhilarating sail and I was moored in the Yealm by mid-afternoon. I was very pleased, I'd found a few problems I could easily sort, such as the cockpit locker leaking and ruining my store of rice and spaghetti. But other than that I'd proved that we could handle conditions that a lot of leisure sailors would struggle with.

And now here we were, moored up safely in yet another tranquil and beautiful haven.

The following day I spent some time drying things out and tidying the boat before rowing ashore to explore. I walked down the footpath along Newton Creek to the little village of Newton Ferrers. The whole place was picture postcard material: The river within a deeply wooded valley. Boats on moorings. Pretty thatched riverside cottages with perfectly tended gardens sloping down to the waters edge. And a beautiful old pub called The Dolphin Inn.

I treated myself to a pint there which I drank in the warm sunshine taking in the view.

After a bit of a siesta back on 'Mor Gwas,' I rowed to the other side of the river and walked through the woods to Noss Mayo on the opposite bank to Newton Ferrers. Huddled around Noss Creek, the place just oozed character with its 'olde worlde' cottages, little quays and stone walls, it was gorgeous.

As I sat in the cockpit that evening the only sounds were gentle lapping water and the haunting echoes of Curlews. I slept very peacefully.

In what was now becoming a monotonous routine, the weather turned bad again. Gale force winds and heavy rain swept in, so I ended up spending another week in the Yealm.

In actual fact, the weather was freakish for early May and one night saw F9/ 10 gusts blowing down the river. 'Mor Gwas' heeled and veered around her mooring and in the morning I found the dinghy which had been tethered astern had flipped over. I was truly weather-bound and the harbourmaster decently waived his mooring fees for which I was grateful.

The delay at least gave me a chance to explore the coastal paths round and about. I walked around Wembury Bay as far as The Mewstone from where I could see the whole of Plymouth Sound and out as far as The Eddystone 12nm away.

On another day, I walked in the opposite direction to Yealm Head. I saw a grass snake, a cormorant struggling to swallow an eel, big silver jumping fish and skylarks.

I'd got chatting with a nice couple from the Trimaran 'Scotch Mist' which was moored close to 'Mor Gwas'. I'd met Brian on the landing slip one morning and he was particularly interested in 'Mor Gwas'.

In his youth, he had owned a Caprice like Shane's 'Shrimpy' and lived aboard. It was great to meet someone who understood what I was doing. Most folks just looked incredulous when I told them I lived aboard that little boat on the mooring.

Brian invited me aboard 'Scotch Mist' for coffee. His wife Lynne, a Kiwi, was a painter and sold watercolours of local scenes to supplement their income. 'Scotch Mist' was some 45ft long and 20 odd feet wide, but all the accommodation lay within the slender central hull. It was really quite small for a big boat, but Brian and Lynne had lived aboard for years very happily, sailing back and forth along the South Coast. I was beginning to realise that I wasn't the first to escape from normality.

My time in the Yealm was very enjoyable, but I'd been there a week and the last leg of my journey awaited. Falmouth lay a day sail away down the coast and I was eager to get going.

It was Saturday 14th May when I finally cleared the Yealm and sailed out towards the Eddystone. Conditions were perfect with a SE 3/ 4, good visibility and clear sky. I got the self-steering working, I saw dolphins, I relaxed in the cockpit with a cup of tea, I felt completely at home.

Just before seven in the evening Pendennis Castle hove into view and I came round St Anthony Head into the Carrick Roads and Falmouth. A month before I'd nervously sailed out of Portsmouth harbour a complete novice. But now I was here, I'd safely navigated my way along the South Coast, I'd negotiated Portland Bill, I'd been baptised as a single-handed sailor.

It was emotional, and the salt water in my eyes wasn't all from the sea. I was so happy to have achieved my goal, but it was happiness tinged with sadness. I had no one to share my joy with.

6

Penryn

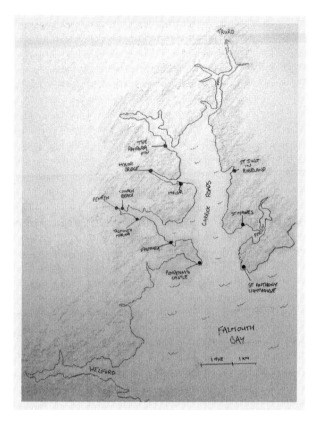

Falmouth Area

AFTER A NIGHT SPENT on a mooring near Falmouth Town Quay, I motored up river towards the town of Penryn.

I'd got it in mind to see if I could find a berth in a place called Sailors Creek on the Flushing side. I remembered reading that Shane Acton had kept 'Shrimpy' there before leaving on his round the world trip. With no other ideas about where to go I figured it was worth a look.

It didn't take long to get there but as I nosed 'Mor Gwas' into the Creek things looked bleak. There were about half a dozen old boats moored on the banks at either side, most were in a poor state of repair. Some had been abandoned, a few had old tarpaulins lashed over them.

But it was obvious that there were also folks living here as wood smoke chuffed out of chimneys on some. Between these semi-floating derelicts, the muddy ribs of once proud vessels could be seen sticking up out of the water. The shoreline was littered with old timbers, rusty old steel and rubbish. It was grey and raining quite hard and compared to the beautiful spots where I'd been moored over the previous weeks it looked like hell. I didn't hang around and headed further up the river to Penryn.

With my plan A out of the window I needed a Plan B. Once I got a little farther up river I put 'Mor Gwas' on a vacant mooring. After pumping up the dinghy I rowed over to the quay. I wanted to find the harbourmasters office. If there was going to be anywhere to get 'Mor Gwas' berthed then he'd be the man to know.

The harbourmaster was friendly and helpful and half an hour later I was sorted. It cost me the princely sum of £10 for rights to 1 years mooring on Church Beach on the other side of the river. It dried at low tide, I'd have to lay out my own stern anchors in the mud and tie the bow up to trees but it was sheltered and it'd do.

Now the word beach is perhaps a tad misleading here, because apart from a few feet of firm shingle near the bank it was all soft mud. I was to get very familiar with Penryn river mud over the coming days and months. I squelched out in it to dig in two big boulders to secure my stern lines. Over the course of a week, I squelched through it to build a little stone causeway so that I could get aboard at low tide without sinking into a foot of it. I squelched through it to clean off the hull and work on the rubbing strakes, and I squelched through it every time I wanted to get ashore at low tide. There wasn't a day went by that I didn't get mud where I didn't want mud to be.

At one point I even rigged up a rope so that I could climb/ abseil up and down the steep rocky bank in front of my berth to reach the footpath higher up. This meant I could avoid the muddy walk along the 'beach'. But all I ever did was reduce the amount coming aboard, I never stopped it.

I soon started to feel at home though, finding my way around and generally making life more comfortable. The vicar of St Gluvias Church at the head of the Creek gave me permission to use the tap in the churchyard for fresh water and washing off my boots.

Penryn town was a short walk away and I set up a mail forwarding address at the Post Office. Plus I could walk to Falmouth in about 30 minutes.

My goal had been to get here and here I was but now what?

The following weeks were quite tough, the weather turned unseasonably cold wet and windy yet again. Everything was damp. Stuff was muddy, and I slashed one of the dinghy tubes on some broken glass hidden in the mud which meant I couldn't get on or off the boat at high water.

My mood matched the weather and I felt a little lost.

For the past few months I'd had clear goals of getting 'Mor Gwas' ready for sea, learning to sail and getting to Falmouth, now I needed another challenge.

My finances were non-existent and I was pretty much surviving on the tinned food I'd stocked the boat with. I'd been looking for work without success. There wasn't much on offer to be fair. I did briefly considered taking the position of part-time pasty crimper at the W.C. Rowes factory. It would have looked great on my C.V.

But as things got desperate I decided to sign on for unemployment benefit. This depressed me even more as I felt like I'd failed. How could I even consider sailing full-time if I couldn't support myself?

I was determined it'd only be a short term measure though and I kept looking.

I walked miles most days, exploring the area, thinking as I walked and trying to lighten my mood.

There were quite a few liveaboards on Church Beach in a fascinating variety of craft. I'd not met many of them yet other than to shout 'good morning' as we rushed past each other in the wind and rain. But as the weather improved folks started spending more time outdoors and I got to know them better.

One of the characters was Stefan on a huge old barge called 'MFH' which, he told me, was short for 'My Floating Home'. One day I walked down the beach to find a chap climbing up onto 'Sunseeker Of Hamble'. She was a solid looking old Hilliard ketch berthed right next to 'Mor Gwas'.

He introduced himself in a broad Irish accent as Sean and told me he'd just returned after 3 weeks away in Dublin. He invited me aboard for coffee and we chatted for quite a while.

He was preparing 'Sunseeker' to sail down to the Med and I was eager to know more. I didn't know it at the time, but Sean was to be the catalyst for an exciting development.

Over the coming weeks we got to know each other quite well. He'd sold up a cycle hire business in Dublin and was soon to be joined by his girlfriend Paula.

He'd bought 'Sunseeker' the previous year and sailed her down from the Hamble. He'd done a lot of work getting her ship-shape and it seemed to me there was still a lot to do. But he was absolutely adamant that they'd be leaving soon.

With time on my hands I helped him with the many jobs left on his list. Painting and varnishing on deck in the warm sun seemed easy work. In return for my help he often treated me to a pub meal and a few pints.

Not only that but we agreed that as long as I helped him take 'Sunseeker' down to the Marina to fill the water tanks now and again I could use his onboard shower.

For me that was the ultimate in luxury after my all over flannel washes in the cockpit.

Over a pint one night Sean happened to mention that during his time in Falmouth he'd been doing some work as crew for a yacht delivery skipper. His name was Clive Phillips and he ran a one-man business called 'Comfort Marine'.

He'd been paying Sean £10 per day all found to help him deliver yachts around the place.

To be honest, I had no idea that yacht delivery companies even existed. In fact, I wasn't even sure what yacht delivery was.

Anyway with Sean leaving Clive was now looking for someone else to crew for him now and again, was that something I'd be interested in? I didn't hesitate. I said "yeah for sure".

A few days later I was down below tatting about when there was a knock on the hull and I heard Seans voice calling my name.

I popped up on deck and saw Sean standing on the beach next to a giant of a man wearing a Breton cap and a Fishermans sweater, I guessed I was about to meet Clive.

It was absurd to consider inviting them aboard. 'Mor Gwas'' cockpit might just have accommodated Sean and me, but there was no way Clive would have fitted. So we hopped aboard 'Sunseeker' and while Paula put the coffee on we sat down to chat.

Clive was fascinated to hear about my trip down from the Solent. I was wary that he would think me reckless and stupid to have attempted the trip but no, he was quite complimentary and even praised my choice of boat.

It turned out he'd once owned a Hurley 22 which was a slightly larger version of 'Mor Gwas'. When the coffee arrived we all continued to yarn for a while as sailors round a table tend to do and as we parted company Clive said he'd be in touch.

I wasn't sure what that meant, Sean reckoned Clive liked me and hinted that if he hadn't I'd have known about it. I was to find out later what that meant.

I put our chat into the back of my mind and pretty much forgot about it.

As June progressed I made more improvements to 'Mor Gwas'.

In particular, I knocked through from the cabin into one of the stern lockers and created a quarter berth that would be far more comfortable to use at sea.

I sailed often, exploring The Helford, The Fal and The Carrick Roads and I continued to help Sean and Paula with their preparations.

The days passed without drama except for one crazy incident. I was in the cockpit one afternoon when I noticed that an old tug called 'Humphrey Morris' had started to move.

She'd been moored alongside Islington Wharf at the head of the river since I'd arrived. She pulled away from the quay and began turning then stopped dead. She was almost as long as the river was wide and I reckoned she'd got her bow stuck in the mud near the bank.

Anyway, the skipper decided that he'd use the tugs not inconsiderable horsepower to get her free, so he opened the throttles. Black smoke belched from her funnel, the water churned up from her stern mixed with what must have been tons of mud.

Now Penryn river is effectively a dead end at Islington Wharf so all this water and mud was forced back down the river towards us. I watched with amazement as this brown mini tsunami came racing down towards 'Mor Gwas'.

Folks started appearing on deck as their boats started rocking and in some cases drifting towards each other. As the mass of fast moving water and mud hit 'Mor Gwas' side on I saw my stern lines go slack and we started swinging towards 'Sunseeker' downstream.

My anchors had been ripped out of the mud. Luckily Sean was

on deck and between us we managed to fend off and avoid damage.

In the meantime 'Humphrey Morris' had freed herself and was moving downriver. She was sent on her way by shouts of abuse from many badly shaken liveaboards, me included.

At 2 the next morning I, along with many others, were squelching in the mud relaying anchors still cursing the skipper of the 'Humphrey Morris'.

Other memorable days included sailing out to see the start of the Azores and Back (AZAB) race. The highlight of which was seeing '3M Mariner'. She was a junk-rigged Coromandel about the same size and a similar design to 'Mor Gwas' and sailed single-handed by a guy called Mike Spring.

The fact that he completed the race is achievement enough but Mike is paraplegic. It made my own achievement seem insignificant. But at the same time bolstering my determination to take 'Mor Gwas' ocean sailing. If Mike could do it I had no excuse.

Towards the end of June Sean and Paula took 'Sunseeker' down to a mooring in Falmouth to make final preparations for departure. And I found myself spending more and more time helping them.

I'd worked on Survival Equipment during my time in the Royal Navy so I was able to service their liferaft. I went up the mast to repair navigation lights, I serviced their engine, stripped and greased winches, the list just went on. All three of us worked hard all day then in the evening we'd usually find ourselves in The Chainlocker for a few pints and a meal. The sun shone and life was good.

One evening the delivery skipper Clive and his wife Jean joined us. Clive regaled us with tales of his most recent trips to Spain and Portugal and hinted that he may well have need of some crew soon. I could only keep my fingers crossed.

We put 'Sunseeker' on the large concrete slipway down at Seahawk boats and scrubbed her off between tides. The following day we got another coat of anti-foul on. Sean was starting to get frustrated as his planned departure date drew nearer and the list of jobs seemed to be never ending. Tempers started to fray and I was tempted to leave him to it a few times, but I couldn't do it.

Finally though on 27th June 'Sunseeker' was ready and I bought 'Mor Gwas' down river so that I could sail out into the bay and see them off. It was a balmy late evening when we cast off from the moorings and drifted slowly out into the Carrick Roads, out past Black Rock and into the Bay. A gentle Northerly breeze pushed us along nicely, it was warm, the sky was crystal clear and the stars formed a glittering canopy overhead. A huge red harvest moon hung low on the horizon. And to complete this out of world experience the water glowed with the brightest phosphorescence I'd ever seen. Sparkling green points of light danced around the hulls of both boats and back into our wakes. I leaned over the side of the cockpit and lifted a handful of water. It flowed through my fingers like liquid moonlight. It was magical.

As we drew abeam of the Helford and knowing I faced a slow sail back to Falmouth, I waved goodbye. As I beat back against the warm gentle breeze I kept glancing over my shoulder until their masthead light disappeared. I was tempted to turn back around and follow them, but I knew I wasn't ready. I was on my own again, but now I could re-focus and I knew that soon I'd be following them South.

It was odd when I got 'Mor Gwas' back to the Beach. Over the next few days I started feeling a little lonely as I sat on 'Mor Gwas' looking at the empty mud berth where 'Sunseeker' had been. It's a funny thing, when a boat has been taking the ground on a mud berth for any length of time the mud gets formed into an impression of the keel and the hull. With the boat gone each low tide reveals the imprint, like a memory. And, if the boat doesn't return, like a memory the imprint gradually fades with time and each turn of the tide. Eventually no trace remains.

A few weeks later I got a postcard from them. They'd had a rough crossing of Biscay but they'd made it to Vigo in Northern Spain and all was well. I knew it would be.

July was a scorcher, for day after day the sun shone and it was hot. I split my time between working on 'Mor Gwas' and sailing and there was nothing I wanted more.

One afternoon while sitting in the cockpit enjoying a cold drink, I spotted one of the little hire boats from Custom House Quay pottering up the river towards me. It was unusual to see one of these little cabin cruisers so far up a drying river, not least with a fast ebbing tide. As the boat got closer it headed away from the deep water channel and across what I knew to be a big mud bank.

The next thing I heard was the outboard engine screaming as it kicked up out of the water and stopped. Through the binoculars I could see the folks onboard looking quizzically over the side of the boat. It only took a few minutes before even they could see the problem as a sea of mud appeared all around the boat.

It seemed that no one else had seen their predicament so I jumped off 'Mor Gwas' and walked down the beach to within shouting distance. There was a man, his wife, two small children and a dog aboard and as soon as they spotted me they started waving and shouting for help. The guy wanted me to phone the lifeboat to get them off. The boat was aground about 25 yards off the beach. I knew for a fact that the mud was only about a foot deep so I told him his best option was to throw out the boats anchor and wade ashore.

He didn't seem keen, I could see that the kids and his wife were getting upset so I took pity, walked back to 'Mor Gwas' for my wellies and waded out to them. The guy was cursing the boat hire chappy because he'd told them that there was always water in the Fal. I pointed out that he was in fact in the Penryn river not the Fal, but he wasn't listening.

Anyway, I laid out the anchor then piggybacked the two children ashore before going back to help his good lady. She seemed less than impressed at wading through the mud in her bare feet. Her husband nearly ended up face first in it as he tried to wade through the glutinous mud with a labrador on his shoulders. Once ashore I led them back down the beach to the Churchyard so they could wash off with the tap. I then showed them the phone box so they could ring a taxi to get back to Falmouth.

His wife was very thankful, but he just grunted. As they say in Cornwall ……. Emmets!

August rolled in and I was happy, I had a goal, work on 'Mor Gwas' was progressing well and the weather held, then a letter arrived. I'd walked up to the Post Office to collect my mail and had been pleased to see that there was a letter from my Dad. I always looked forward to letters from home and as usual I took it back to the boat to read over a coffee.

My heart sank as I read the contents, my Mom had been admitted to hospital suffering from chronic depression. She'd suffered for years but this was a dramatic turn of events and I needed to find out more. I jogged down the beach to the phone box and got hold of Dad at his office. I could tell immediately that things were bad. Before I got the chance to ask about Mom he told me that my brother Andy had suffered a serious cycling accident in the French Alps. He was being airlifted back to the UK. He'd come off his bike descending a steep mountain pass and gone over the edge. All Dad knew was that he had several broken bones and concussion.

Mom was in a hospital in Northampton which was 100 mile round trip from Dads place. He was driving there every night after work and he didn't yet know where Andy was going to be. For obvious reasons Mom hadn't been told about Andy's accident. I knew what I had to do. 'Mor Gwas' would have to look after herself for a while, duty called.

I was up country for nearly three weeks doing what I could to help. It was odd sleeping in my old bedroom, living on the land again. The luxury of hot baths and showers, electricity, proper meals eaten at a table. The novelty soon wore off though and I began to realise that I'd changed.

I now valued different things.

As the days passed and things improved with Mom and Andy my desire to get back to 'Mor Gwas' grew stronger and in late

August I got the train back to Cornwall. Back to my little boat in the mud, my home.

It took me a while to settle into life aboard again but not as long as I'd expected. Ridiculous though it may sound this tiny fibreglass tub really did feel like home now.

My thoughts soon turned back to my planned voyage and I picked up where I'd left off with preparing 'Mor Gwas' although now the urgency had faded. I'd lost most of August up country and there was no way I was going to be ready in the next few weeks.

While I'd been away I'd been thinking about my destination and I'd decided on Northern Spain.

Maybe I should have considered a Channel hop over to France or The Channel Islands first but I wanted to push myself. In some respects ocean sailing was easier. Remember that back then GPS was still a new technology and very expensive. There was no way I could afford this luxury so I was relying on the traditional methods. I'd be using a trailing Walker log, a plastic sextant and paper charts. My skill and confidence had grown in the trip down from Portsmouth. But I didn't yet feel ready to tackle the notoriously difficult coasts around that part of the world.

I'd learned enough to know that it's the hard rocky bits where most yachts come to grief not the lumpy wet bits.

Of course getting to Northern Spain meant I'd have to cross The Bay of Biscay. I was under no illusions, crossing the Bay meant exposing 'Mor Gwas' and me to the Atlantic, it would be ocean sailing for sure.

A few days later as I was walking back down the beach after a trip into Falmouth I happened to glance across to the quay. To my surprise saw another Silhouette tied up alongside.

She was an older MkII of timber construction (' Mor Gwas' was a glass fibre MkIII). Later that evening I could see that there was someone aboard so I strolled round to have a chat.

The guy introduced himself as Dave and invited me aboard for a cuppa.

Now despite the extra fitting out I'd done to make 'Mor Gwas' more comfortable I still thought of her as being pretty basic. But 'Sea Elf' as Dave's boat was called was really basic. In fact she was just a cabin. He had a hurricane lamp for lighting and like me a Primus stove for cooking but apart from a foam mattress, a sleeping bag and a few books that seemed about it. Dave seemed very happy with her though and as I was to discover he had good reason to feel like he was living in luxury.

Dave came from Lancashire. He'd set out from Merseyside somewhere some months before in an Enterprise open sailing dinghy to sail down to Cornwall. To be honest I didn't believe him, but as he told me about the trip I started to realise that it must be true, it would have been impossible to make it up.

He'd day sailed and each evening had fetched up somewhere, thrown a tarp over the boom and kipped down in his sleeping bag. He'd lived on corned beef and potatoes. He'd drifted into a coastal firing range somewhere off the North Wales coast and had to be towed clear. He'd been 'rescued' many times when the wind dropped but somehow had made it as far as Padstow on the North Cornish coast.

By the time he'd got there he was in a bad way and had been hospitalised suffering from trench foot. Apparently he'd met up with one of the locals in a pub one night who was so appalled at what he'd been through he just gave him 'Sea Elf'.

With a roof over his head he was like a dog with two tails and had carried on his journey and had arrived only today. Now let's not be under any illusions here. Dave was probably suffering from some sort of mental problem or breakdown. He was for all intents and purposes living as a tramp.

But as I was to discover over the coming months his attitude to life and people in general was unlike anyone I'd ever met.

As long as he had some baccy for his pipe, a mug of tea, some potatoes to eat and a roof over his head he was a king.

I never saw him without a big grin on his face and his cheery Lancastrian accent always went down well. He was one of these guys who could get away with things most of us couldn't and more than that would do things most of us wouldn't.

One small example, some weeks later we were both walking into Falmouth on what it has to be said was a foul day. It was cold wet and windy. Coming towards us was a middle-aged woman pulling a shopping trolley. She had a scarf wrapped tightly over her head and was walking quickly towards us head down. The look on her face would have curdled milk.

Dave deliberately walked straight towards her, changing direction when she did until she was forced to stop as he blocked her way. She lifted her head with anger on her face and no doubt some abuse about to cross her lips.

All she saw was Dave's huge grin beaming through his bushy grey beard.

"Ey up me love, what's with the grim face? I bet you've got a lovely smile under there somewhere" Dave said.

To my utter amazement her face transformed as the corners of her mouth curled upwards into a smirk. "There I knew I were right, that's much better" he said, as he stepped out of her way and doffed the flat cap he always wore.

She set off again and after a few steps glanced back, the smile still on her lips.

I shook my head and looked at Dave in disbelief. He may have had no money and hardly any possessions, but he, had something I for one consider far more valuable.

7

Autonomy

SOME WEEKS later I'd pretty much decided I wouldn't see Clive again. But one day, to my surprise, I looked up to see his unmistakable figure striding down the shingle towards the boat.

I was pleased to see him and invited him aboard for a coffee.

As he grabbed the bowsprit and hauled himself up onto the rope ladder leading to the foredeck I thought 'Mor Gwas' would tilt forward on her keels. He seemed even bigger as he squeezed himself down the side deck and eased himself down in the cockpit.

While the kettle was boiling, we started chatting and he asked me what I had planned for the next week. To be honest I didn't need to go below and fetch my diary, the answer tripped straight off my tongue "not a lot".

"Good" he replied, "get yourself down to Falmouth Marina early doors on Monday and bring kit for a couple of nights, we've got a milk run up to the Solent to do".

I tried to keep cool as I nodded and said "great" but I suspect my excitement showed through as I asked more about the job. Clive went on to tell me that it involved delivering a 36ft Admirals Cup racing yacht back to Lymington.

He referred to these trips as milk runs because they were so common. Falmouth seemed to be the terminus for many a Londoner's trip down the South Coast before they ran out of holiday time and had to head back.

Once home they picked up the phone to Clive and asked him to get their boat back to them ASAP.

I couldn't believe it, the idea of owning a beautiful sailboat but not having the time to sail her seemed alien to me. I soon found out though that it's the norm, not the exception.

The boat we took up to the Solent was called 'Autonomy'. As we motored out past Falmouth docks Clive told me a bit about her.

Apparently she'd been knocked about a bit during the infamous Fastnet race of 1979 and had subsequently been completely re-fitted.

Being aboard her was a whole new experience for me, she seemed huge both above and below decks with her wide beam and giant winches. I had butterflies as Clive pointed her into the wind and called on me to haul up the main, but I needn't have worried. It's a beautiful thing that the principles of sail and sailing remain the pretty much the same whatever boat you're on. You just need to find the right bit of rope, haul on it and find some wind.

Sailors will tell you that sailing consists of short bursts of frenetic activity followed by long spells of doing very little. This trip proved the rule.

Once we'd made sail and set a course towards the Eddystone Clive switched on the autopilot and I went below to put the kettle on.

The wind was a decent Force 4 and forward of the beam so 'Autonomy' was heeling quite well. I found it scary having so much space on the 'downhill' side. On 'Mor Gwas,' I almost didn't need to hold on down below because even if I slipped I couldn't go very far. 'Autonomy' was different and I kept a hand for myself.

We were storming along at 8 knots and Clive was happy. He wanted to get this delivery out of the way because he'd taken on a big job that he was keen to get started on. There was a boat in

Falmouth Marina called 'Abraxis' that the owner wanted converting to Chinese junk rig.

Clive had taken on the job of overseeing the work and then delivering her to Tenerife before Christmas. He said nothing about needing crew and I didn't dare ask, but I couldn't help getting excited at the possibility that I might get a chance.

Sadly though our speedy progress on 'Autonomy' didn't last. After a couple of hours the wind died and the engine came back on. I don't like motoring on sailboats. They're noisy, the exhaust fumes always seem to end up in the cockpit and the whole boat vibrates as the prop turns. Being a racing boat she had a small engine which meant the revs were high. The now departed breeze had left a messy chop.

'Autonomy' would climb up the advancing waves before dropping back into the trough. When that happened she slamming her saucer-shaped bottom hard onto the water. It was very uncomfortable and it struck me that I'd much prefer to be on 'Mor Gwas' in these conditions than this multi-thousand-pound vessel.

We'd left Falmouth Marina at 0900 and it was now 1900 and Start Point was on the nose. Given the lack of wind, the uncomfortable conditions and our rapidly depleting fuel supply. Not to mention our need for a beer. Clive decided we'd overnight in Salcombe.

He was big mates with some of the guys at the Island Cruising Club. They had an ex-Mersey ferry called 'Egremont' moored in the harbour. 'Egremont' was used as an accommodation and training vessel and we had a very pleasant evening there.

Highlights included a fast, torch-lit RIB trip up the river to a pub where we finally got our long-awaited pint or two.

The following morning, after filling up with diesel, we departed about 0900 and resumed our trip.

An uneventful sail across Lyme Bay saw us off Portland at 1900 although we didn't see it. We were well offshore to avoid The Race and I couldn't help but draw comparisons with the last time I'd passed this way aboard 'Mor Gwas' some 6 months before.

Then I was still learning to sail, and now here I was working as 'professional' yacht crew, well I hoped so at least. I thought I'd done my job pretty well so far and I hoped Clive thought the same, I wanted more of this. Not long after we'd cleared Portland and with darkness and fog descending we began picked up the unmistakable stench of diesel fuel. It kept getting stronger and after an initial panic that it was coming from 'Autonomy' we realised that we'd sailed into a floating slick of it.

Clive said it wasn't unusual to come across this sort of pollution in The Channel. The huge volume of commercial shipping passing back and forth every day made it somewhat inevitable. But after half an hour or so we were still sailing through it and we realised that this was something different.

Our throats were beginning to burn: The fumes were that strong. At one point, we put our handkerchiefs over our faces to try and afford some protection. Clive went down below to get on the VHF and report it. When he came back he told me that the coastguard were aware and that pollution control vessels were on their way.

There had been a collision between a Royal Naval Vessel, HMS 'Fearless'. And a German Bulk Freighter called 'Gerhardt', that's where the fuel had come from. We later found out that 'Gerhardt' had been rammed amidships and virtually cut in two.

Miraculously there were no serious injuries.

It was a little worrying to be aboard a small sailing vessel in an area frequented by large ships, at night and with the fog getting thicker. If two large ships like this could collide what chance did we have of being seen.

The answer was none.

All we could do was strain our eyes and ears and keep our fingers crossed.

We put the engine back on and motor-sailed the rest of the way. We were tired and 'Autonomy' seemed to be tiring too. Over the course of the next few hours the gas ran out, the pressurised water system failed, the VHF radio became intermittent, the log stopped working, and the radio direction finder packed up. Luckily we knew that if we kept our heading we'd be able to pick up the Needles Light alright, but losing these navigation aids in such poor conditions wasn't ideal.

Just to add to the fun all the chocks holding the keel stepped mast tight where it passed through the coachroof fell out. This left the mast wobbling about like a stick in a bucket.

I carefully replaced them with a big hammer.

At 0330 we were heading past Hurst Point ready to turn to port into the Lymington Channel.

It was really foggy closer inshore. I ended up in the pulpit with a big torch trying to spot the channel markers so that I could shout instructions back to Clive on the helm.

It had been a long day and we were mighty pleased to tie up alongside at the Berthon Marina at 0430.

After a few hours sleep, we jumped ship and headed to the railway station. I slept pretty much all the way back and did most of the trip on my own.

This was because Clive got off at Salisbury to buy some coffee and bacon rolls and didn't make it back to the train before it pulled out of the station.

The first I knew was when I woke with a start as the train jolted and started to move. I looked around the compartment wondering where Clive was. Then looked out of the window to see him standing on the end of the platform with two cups of coffee in his outstretched hands and two bacon rolls in his mouth.

It's probably a good thing his mouth was full.

I had to wait an hour and a half at Truro station for him to arrive on the next train.

He was still fuming.

8

Abraxis

WE'D HAD A LONG TRIP, and were both pretty tired. Clive was still short tempered by the time we got back to his place in Mylor. As soon as we arrived he asked Jean, his wife, to run me back to Penryn saying he'd be in touch. To be honest, I had no idea whether I'd impressed him enough to be crewing for him again let alone on 'Abraxis'. But I knew I'd done the best I could.

The 'Autonomy' trip had undoubtedly been a good test and I thought I'd done OK, but I'd just have to see what happened. As it turned out I didn't have to wait long. The following morning there was a loud knock on the hull and the sound of Clive's now cheery voice. "Come on you lazy arse, we've got a boat to get ready for sea". It seemed I'd passed the test.

As Clive drove me down to the marina he told me that he'd pay me £ 2 per hour for working on 'Abraxis' before we left and £ 10 per day for the time we were at sea. This was all found and with all travel expenses covered. 'Abraxis' had to be in Tenerife by early December at the absolute latest and we had a shed load of work to do before we could leave. I couldn't believe it. The best I'd hoped for was another 'milk run'. But now I had paid work doing something I loved and I was going to sail to the Canary Islands. I felt, quite literally that my ship had come in.

As I walked down the pontoon towards 'Abraxis' I was excited, but my first sight of her took the edge off my enthusiasm somewhat. I began to wonder what I'd let myself in for.

'Abraxis' was unlike any yacht I'd ever seen. Clive had already told me that the boat was being converted to Chinese Junk rig but the only work that had been done so far was to replace the masts. There was no mistaking her. Not least because her hull was painted matt black. In stark contrast the shiny new unstayed masts stuck up into the sky like big giant needles.

Clive filled me in with some more detail. 'Abrades' was steel hulled and originally built in Holland in the 1930' s. Her owner was a gentleman by the name of Mike Pratt, apparently a professor of accountancy (who knew there was such a thing).

He was living in South Africa from where he would be sending instructions to Clive. Mike had negotiated a sabbatical from the University he lectured at and would be arriving in Tenerife early December with his wife and baby. From there they planned to sail the Atlantic to Antigua.

On the face of it, our job was very simple, Mike had already ordered the sails, running rigging and various other bits and pieces. All we had to do was coordinate with the various suppliers and tradesmen to ensure everything was fitted correctly.

In the meantime we'd carry out a complete overhaul of the boat in general, do the sea-trials and then deliver her to Tenerife.

Clive made it sound easy.

The timetable meant we had four to five weeks maximum to get everything done. Clive wanted to get away in early November so to give us the best chance of half decent weather across Biscay. That would also give us some time in hand in case of problems en-route.

I was learning that the yacht delivery business is just that, a business. It differs hugely from sailing for pleasure because there are contracts and timetables to keep. There had to be a balance of course, safety still took priority. That aside though Clive took pride in never having failed to get a vessel where it was wanted when it was wanted.

The following weeks sped past in a seemingly constant flurry of activity. Inevitably there were problems, in fact, there were quite a lot of problems. As it turned out the owner hadn't set foot on 'Abraxis' for a couple of years. About six months previously he'd decided that he wanted to go sailing again and that he fancied converting 'Abraxis' to Junk Rig. Being an academic, he'd done endless research into the subject before ordering all the necessary components. But given the number of different suppliers and that everything had been done remotely it was inevitable things wouldn't go smoothly.

There was hardly a day went by that Clive didn't spend time on the phone to South Africa. And, Clive being Clive, hardly a day went by when he didn't end up shouting at someone.

But gradually we began to get 'Abraxis' ship-shape. Anyone who knows anything about Chinese Junk rig will tell you that there's one thing in particular that makes them different from other types of sailing rigs. It's the sheer amount of rope needed to control the sails.

A junk rig sail is a little like a window blind with a number of horizontal battens dividing the sail up into panels. Each of these battens has its own sheet or control line, add in the halyards and you end up with metres and metres of rope.

'Abraxis' was schooner rigged. That meant here was two of everything. Mike had ordered coils of nasty polypropylene stuff that twisted and kinked when you so much as looked at it. All this rope had to be led back to the steering position at the stern. Here there was an internal seat and a round hatch through which the helmsman could see all round.

This meant that dozens of metal eyes had to be welded to the deck so that blocks and pulleys could be attached.

Clive and I spent hours working out what went where. We marked the positions on deck and then tried to establish where the corresponding position was inside the boat. We needed to do this so that we could remove panelling and trim and make sure nothing caught fire when Gerry the welder welded the eye in position.

We still needed the fire extinguisher now and again though. Come to think about it, we used fire extinguishers quite a lot on 'Abraxis'. Not only during the welding but when we tested the paraffin cooker (it was faulty) and once at sea (more on that later).

Finally, once we got all the eyes, blocks, fairleads and cleats fitted it was time to get the sails on. Thankfully it was a calm and dry morning when two sailmakers turned up to do the job.

It took the bulk of the day getting them lashed on. Mike had sent Clive reams of instructions and design drawings. But as neither we nor the sailmakers had any experience with junk rig we were all in unknown territory.

There were more than a few trips up the masts and much cussing and cursing over kinked and fouled rope. By the end of the afternoon though we had two sails hauled up and 'Abraxis' was attracting even more attention.

There were plenty of other 'firsts' for us as well. Mike was an enthusiastic radio amateur and there was a huge transmitter/receiver fitted in the stern compartment. One of the many deliveries we received was a huge fibreglass antenna some 20 feet long which Mike had instructed should be fitted to the transom. This caused us no end of grief.

It was unwieldy and heavy, we mocked up a substantial mounting bracket using timber which looked OK and then got Gerry to fabricate it out of steel. We then had a fun couple of hours trying to get it welded into position. This involved muggins balancing in a dinghy holding it above my head.

With Clive lying on the pontoon steadying it, Gerry hung over the stern trying to weld it in place.

It's a good job 'Abraxis' had a hard tender as molten metal dripping onto an inflatable dinghy would probably have caused some problems.

As it was I ended up with a singed bobble hat.

Once the job was finished 'Abraxis' resembled some strange insect. The giant aerial looking like a huge stinger protruding up from its arse.

Other unusual jobs included the fabrication and fitting of a revolving pram hood over the aft observation hatch. Also fitting a dozen canvas bags around the cockpit to hold all the loose ends of sail control lines.

'Abraxis' was now starting to draw all sorts of attention.

Apart from her strange appearance there was constant activity aboard. Welders, sailmakers, electronics engineer, upholsterers, carpenter, even a carpet fitter. Not only that but it was now well known that she was bound for The Canaries and West Indies.

One morning a young lady from Radio Cornwall arrived along with a sound engineer. They spent an hour on board interviewing Clive about the boat and the trip. As 'first mate,' I got in on the act as well but I have no idea if any of our rabbiting was ever broadcast.

These were happy days, every day was a new challenge and we were working towards an exciting voyage. Even the weather seemed to be holding out and not only that I'd fallen in love.

Her name was Mary, dark hair, blue eyes, and an enthusiastic sailor. She appeared on the pontoon one day looking for Clive as she was interested in crewing for him. Clive had nipped into town for some bits and pieces so I invited her aboard for a coffee while she waited.

We hit it off straight away and she seemed very impressed with my adventures on 'Mor Gwas'. I think she thought I was winding her up when I said I lived aboard though.

We spent a bit of time together over the next few weeks and it was fun, but it was never going to go anywhere. She lived in a big house over at Restronguet Point (super posh) and mixed with the Falmouth racing crowd at The Royal Cornwall Yacht Club.

I was a poor boy boat bum living in the mud.

Clive asked me if he should perhaps invite her to come on the

Tenerife trip with us, I said no, not if he wanted me to keep my mind on the sailing. If you're out there Mary, I'm sorry.

Work continued apace and towards the end of October we were finally ready for some sea trials.

We moved 'Abraxis' down to a mooring off Falmouth town. From there we could easily nip out into The Carrick Roads for a few hours when we wanted to play with something.

We fitted, setup and tested the electronic autopilot. Mounted the steering compass and had it swung, and, of course, tried sailing for the first time.

After the first few attempts, both Clive and I were beginning to think that we'd taken on an impossible job. 'As I said, Abraxis' was rigged as a schooner and getting the sails up was bloody hard work. It wasn't just canvas that needed hauling up, there were a lot of timber battens and rope to go up the masts as well. Even with the winches, it was tough.

Worse, there were also problems bringing the sails down. When the halyard was released the weight of the sail would swing against the mast causing the rope parrels to bind up. It needed Clive and me to hang all our weight off the sails to bring them down and Clive was a big guy. Even then it was a struggle.

The first time we tacked, the mainsail sheets all wrapped around the huge radio antenna we'd spent so long fitting. It was a nightmare.

Adjusting the antenna mounting to give clearance was fairly straight forward. But we absolutely had to sort out the problem with hauling the sails up and down. Unbelievably the answer was beeswax. As we'd discovered, the enemy of junk rig efficiency is friction and eliminating it changed the rig completely. We heavily waxed every piece of rope that came into contact with the mast and tried again. The sails slid up the mast beautifully but more importantly slid down again without a problem.

Gradually Clive and I gained confidence and actually began to appreciate some of the inherent benefits of the rig. We regularly sailed off the mooring. We simply hoisted the sails and with the sheets loose, let them 'weathercock' around the masts, no flogging, no drama, very relaxing.

As the mooring was slipped all that was needed was to sheet in the sails and away we went.

Reefing was a revelation because as I said before, the sails consisted of battened panels. So when we wanted to shorten sail all we needed to do was slacken the halyard. This allowed the sail to drop by however many panels were needed, then the halyard was refastened. The sails had lazy-jacks. This meant no sail ties were needed and in fact, with all the control lines led back to the cockpit it wasn't even necessary to go on deck.

This was something we came to love crossing Biscay. More importantly 'Abraxis' seemed to sail really well. she pointed almost as high as a conventional Bermuda rig, she was fast on a reach, and downwind it was easy to set the sails 'wing-a-wing' without risk of gybing.

It seemed Mr Pratt might have known what he was about after all. The thing that neither of us ever got used to though was the sight of her unstayed masts bending to leeward. We knew that's what they'd been designed to do but none the less it worried us every time we sailed her.

By the 6th November 'Abraxis' was as ready as we could make her. We did a provisioning run, filled up with water and diesel and made ready to depart.

I'd been worried about leaving 'Mor Gwas' at Penryn while I was away. I'd already experienced some petty thievery and she was just too vulnerable to be left there, particularly when the tide was out.

Clive solved the problem as he had a drying mooring right up the river at Mylor Bridge. His boat was out of the water so he suggested I leave 'Mor Gwas' there.

That afternoon on a flood tide I sailed her round Trefusis Point and all the way up the creek. I made her as secure as I could, rigged a tarp over the cockpit and at high water Clive came alongside in the dinghy and off we went.

I knew that it'd be New Year before I stepped back aboard her and as we pulled away it struck me how far we'd come. Not only had she carried me along the South Coast to Falmouth but she'd changed my life in ways I could never have imagined.

It had been an incredible year, but it was going to finish with my biggest adventure yet.

9

The Abraxis Voyage

I'VE LOST the log I kept of our voyage to Tenerife so the following comes straight from memory.

I'm confident it's an accurate and factual recollection though, it was a memorable trip.

We departed Falmouth with a fair wind and good conditions. Clive had been watching the weather looking out for a decent 'window'. The Bay of Biscay has a fearsome reputation and we were leaving late in the season. It's possible to get hammered by the weather there at any time of the year, but we were at greater risk now that Autumn was well established.

I mentioned earlier that delivery skippers generally push things a little more than cruising skippers. So I was a little apprehensive about the trip. That said I had complete faith in the boat and complete faith in Clive. There was even an element of excitement about the possibility of experiencing my first full gale at sea in a small boat.

For the first couple of days out it looked as if I was going to miss out on that experience. Winds were light or non-existent and we did a lot of motoring to stay on schedule. It was during one of these motoring periods that 'Abraxis' slowed down and started to vibrate. Clive knew immediately that we must have fouled the propeller on something.

As we rolled about in the swell we could see a vague dark shape under the water trailing a few feet back from the stern. 'Abraxis' had a long deep keel with a full-length rudder. This meant that the propeller was some 5ft under water and overhung by the transom. There was no way we could get to whatever had caused the problem from the deck.

Someone was going to have to get wet.

There was never any question who that was going to be. I may have been 1st mate, but as the only other person aboard was the Captain I was outranked.

It was about now that I began to wish I had a wetsuit with me.

I got my swim shorts on. Strapped a big diving knife to my calf. Donned mask and snorkel and,with a rope tied round my ankle, jumped overboard.

God knows how many thousand feet of water were underneath me. I tried not to think about it. That was easy to do. When I hit the water the only thought going through my head was 'I'm going to choke on my balls'.

I knew I didn't have time to hang around. My sea survival training told me I'd only got a few minutes to work before hypothermia started taking effect.

I took a breath and dived under the stern. I could see immediately what looked like a big sheet of polyethene wrapped around the prop.

I grabbed a handful and with my feet braced against the rudder, gave it a pull. Luckily most of it came loose but when I dived down again I could see another much tighter piece wrapped around the prop shaft.

It took me three or four attempts sawing madly with the serrated side of the dive knife before I cleared it away.

I was determined to finish the job in one go because the thought of having to jump in again was too much. As a result, I probably stayed in longer than I should have.

'Abraxis' had a permanent steel runged ladder on her transom that should have made it easy to get back aboard. But I still had huge difficulty getting my feet onto the bottom rung and pulling myself up. 'Abraxis' was rolling quite badly and by now I couldn't feel my hands or feet. Somehow I managed it and once I'd got a hold Clive was able to reach down and haul me into the cockpit. He wrapped a big towel around me and helped me down below.

I was shivering uncontrollably and my teeth were chattering so much I'd have lost my tongue if it'd got between them.

Once dry I got in my sleeping bag and Clive kept me supplied with hot tea and, although we ran a dry ship at sea, a hefty tot of Pusser's rum.

Hell, it was good to be warm, and with the prop cleared we continued on our way.

On day three the wind started picking up and for the next 24 hours it continued increasing until it was approaching Force 8. I finally got the experience I'd been waiting for. I thought I knew what to expect.

During my time in the Royal Navy I'd spent a few weeks aboard RFA 'Tidespring' on exercise in The North Sea. During the detachment we'd experienced hurricane force winds, really extreme. I'd seen the aircraft carrier HMS 'Ark Royal' burying her bows in the seas. The Yanks lost an aircraft off the flight deck of one of their huge carriers, washed overboard so rumour said. 'Tidespring' was a big ship. We had two Sea King helicopters aboard. She rolled and buried her bows for sure. But from my perspective working up on the flight deck I was always looking down on the seas.

On 'Abraxis' things were very different. We rose like an express lift to an oncoming swell and then sank just as fast down the other side. The horizon regularly disappeared below towering walls of water. 'Abraxis' seemed very small.

Since leaving Falmouth, we'd gradually become fans of this strange looking junk rigged boat though. Sail handling was an absolute doddle. With no jib to work everything could be done from the safety and comfort of the cockpit. Or as we now started to appreciate, the aft helming position.

The poor weather continued for some 48 hours and during this time neither Clive nor I went on deck once. We never even put our foul weather gear on.

The aft section of 'Abraxis', which we'd named 'The Playpen' was basically a raised section fully upholstered with cushions and backrests. I think it got called the 'The Playpen' after I mentioned that I'd have liked to share a watch or two with Mary in there.

Anyway, it was possible to keep watch there through the observation hatch, using the rotating pram hood canopy to keep the wind and rain off. With all the control lines to hand reefing and sail adjustments could be made without moving from the seat. And with the Autohelm keeping us on course there wasn't much to do other than watch the sea and the sky.

The biggest problem, in fact, was keeping awake because it was so damn comfortable.

With just two of us aboard we were sharing night watches of four hours on four hours off, with the daylight hours shared according to how we felt. It seemed to be working well but by day five as we approached Cape Finisterre we were both starting to feel pretty tired.

Fatigue may have played some part in what was to be one of my most frightening experiences of my life..

After the gale passed the winds dropped lighter. And, as is quite often the case off this part of the Northern Spanish coast, the visibility deteriorated.

Our last estimated position had put us a little way South of Cape Finisterre and 5 or 6 miles offshore.

Clive had told me that he intended to put into Baiona as we needed fuel and both needed rest, the forecast was also looking bad.

I'd learnt a lot about Astronavigation as we crossed the Bay. I'd never used a sextant before and I'd really benefited from Clive's instruction. I'd even overcome my lifelong aversion to anything relating to mathematics which had seemed a major obstacle to working out a position.

But as we'd neared the coast I'd been happy to leave things to Clive. I had complete confidence in him, he'd told me he'd passed this way many times before and knew the approach like the back of his hand.

This overconfidence nearly cost us dear.

As I said, visibility was not great, plus it was a cloudy night with little in the way of moonlight.

We were looking for the flash of a lighthouse that Clive knew lay in the approaches to Baiona.

Clive was using the Decca hand-held direction to try and pick up on coastal radio beacons that could help pinpoint our position. He wasn't having much luck.

The visibility got worse and there seemed to be a smell of smoke in the air. Clive swore it was the smoke from a landfill that he knew lay close to the harbour entrance. He reckoned that the expected light we'd been looking for was being obscured by the mist and smoke.

As we continued into the gloom I suddenly spotted the sweeping loom of a light high above us. Clive saw it too and took it as confirmation we were on the right course. It was eerie watching this blurred beam of light piercing the mist as it swung over the boat and disappeared only to reappear a few seconds later. Despite Clive's confidence, I was worried.

We seemed to be heading straight for the light and my instinct told me that lighthouses are generally put there to warn mariners away, not to draw them in.

I kept quiet though, there could only be one skipper on this boat.

As I strained my eyes ahead I started to see white streaks showing against the darkness. Then almost immediately heard what sounded like distant thunder. Without warning 'Abraxis' seemed to be surrounded by white breaking water. Dark jagged rocks appeared out of the foam like the teeth of some giant monster rising from the depths. Sheer black cliffs appeared right ahead. We were doing 6 knots under sail heading straight for them.

Clive yelled "shit, shit, shit" and span the wheel to starboard as fast as he could. The rig swung round and put us on a reach. As he fired up the engine he yelled at me to get down below and try and identify the light from the chart.

I obeyed without thinking but as I descended the companionway steps I was terrified.

I waited to hear the crash of hard rock against the steel hull. I expected to feel the boat lurch to a halt as jagged rock tore open the hull like a baked bean tin. I could imagine torrents of cold green water gushing into the boat. I could imagine being trapped in a sinking coffin.

I looked down at the chart laid out on the table with not a clue where to start. If we weren't anywhere near the entrance to Baiona then where the hell were we?

I tried to bring to mind the sequence of flashes we'd been watching and then scanned up and down the chart trying to find a light description that matched. It was hopeless, I had to get back on deck. Fear and the boat's motion was making me feel nauseous. Whatever Clive did I simply couldn't stay below, blind to whatever was happening outside.

As I came up through the companionway I could see Clive looking straight ahead. The engine was racing, the sails were weathercocked into the wind and the light was now directly astern and fading back into the gloom. The sea around us was no longer white and foaming. We were safe.

I knew Clive well enough by now not to say anything. I left him at the wheel and went back below to make a brew. After a few minutes I heard the engine revs slow and the engine stopped. As 'Abraxis' heeled I knew the sails were drawing again. I added a few slugs of rum to the mugs of steaming coffee and took them up into the cockpit.

As I handed one to Clive he snapped "did you find that light on the chart?" "No" I answered. He grunted and looked away taking a swig from his mug. "I was damn sure I knew where we were," he said, talking more to himself than me. I said nothing, it wasn't the time for jokes and I could think of nothing sensible to say. We were both in shock, we'd come close to losing the boat and our lives. We both knew what had happened and no words were needed.

We stood offshore for the rest of the night and by morning the visibility had improved. We soon picked out a couple of prominent landmarks and within a few hours we were motoring safely towards Baiona marina.

Clive and I never spoke of that night again. To this day, I don't know where it was that our voyage so nearly ended. I'd learned a priceless lesson though. I'd never again approach land at night without knowing exactly where I was.

We ended up staying in Baiona for about a week as a depression rolled in from the Atlantic. Clive was frustrated by the delay, but I rather enjoyed it.

To be honest, we needed some time apart.

Clive had a temper and when he had one on him the best solution was to avoid him completely.

His navigational error had embarrassed him and he felt he'd lost face. He knew he'd got things wrong and he'd put the boat and lives at risk. It wasn't in his character to apologise though and I wasn't expecting one.

He'd been wound up further by an incident that occurred when we'd arrived and come alongside the marina pontoon.

A little Spanish guy had come running down towards us with a big smile on his face, keen to help us tie up. I was on the bow, and as we pulled up to the pontoon I jumped off to make it fast.

Unseen by Clive the little Spaniard reached onto the stern deck and took the aft line. He pulled it tight to reach the nearest pontoon cleat and as he did so it pulled up under the stern mounted Walker log.

As the line came taut it snapped the log mounting, sending the

Walker log up into a gracefully curved flight. Its trip ended with a splash as it sank into the water.

Clive lost it completely and let rip at the poor guy.

As I've said, Clive was a big guy and with his bushy eyebrows and sideburns protruding from under his Breton cap he could cut a frightening figure. Our little Spanish friend ran away as fast as he could and I can't say I blamed him.

Clive passed away some years ago and I'm reluctant to speak ill. But for all his skill, charm and kindness Clive had a dark side that I saw on many occasions. Sean had warned me he had a temper, but I hadn't been prepared for its intensity. I never saw him use physical violence, but he was skilled in the verbal variety. From what I'd seen it was usually innocent victims that bore the brunt.

The Walker trailing log was one of the most valuable navigational instruments onboard. It was Clive's personal property and he'd used it for many thousands of miles. We should have de-mounted it before coming alongside, but now it was too late. Clive wasn't prepared to lose it though.

A few days later the marina found a diver who, after about 30 minutes of searching, retrieved it from the mud.

Clive stripped, dried and re-lubricated it and it worked perfectly for the rest of the voyage.

I liked Baiona. Once we'd tidied the boat and done a few minor jobs I was pretty much free to explore.

I spent large chunks of the day wandering around the little back streets or walking around the wonderful old castle overlooking the Ria.

Despite the strong winds, the weather stayed generally warm and dry. I loved it. Making landfall on a small boat somehow awakens the senses far more than any other form of transport. The smells in particular. Not all pleasant, but yes, the land has a distinctive odour that those living ashore all the time get used to.

For me, there was also the sub-conscious relief of being safe on terra firma after the drama of a few days before.

The marina in Baiona was quite large and there were yachts from many nations alongside. We got chatting with quite a few folks and I remember several enjoyable evenings spent aboard one boat or another. We shared more than a few sundowners.

It's interesting how the common bond of sailing and the sea draws people together even if there's a language barrier. As a native English speaker I'm all too aware of the advantage we have when travelling. Wherever in the world you go there always seems to be someone around who speaks it. I'm also deeply ashamed of the English lack of foreign language skills. I have some basic French, but that's about it.

Clive embarrassed me often by employing his standard technique for talking to foreigners. His method was simple. Continue using English but at greater and greater volume until it was understood. Bizarrely it seemed to work a lot of the time.

I actually enjoyed trying to communicate in a different language and generally my efforts were appreciated.

I remember one crazy afternoon when I got involved trying to help a German guy on an old Falmouth Pilot boat who's diesel engine had packed up.

I knew a little bit about engines and I'd spent a few hours trying to find out why it wouldn't start but without success.

He was very short of funds, but someone found a Spanish mechanic who said he'd take a look. Now the Spanish guy only spoke Spanish and The German only really spoke German. There was a French guy down the way who spoke Spanish but not German so we found a Belgian who did.

They all spoke some English and as I've said, I had a bit of French.

We all ended up craning our necks peering into the engine compartment while the Spanish mechanic took things apart. He then told the French guy what he'd found. The French guy then told the Belgian guy who did his best to tell the German guy what was going on. I picked up various bits from them all them which I tried to reiterate in French so that French guy could tell the mechanic.

If ever there was an opportunity for information to be lost in translation then this was it. Somehow though after a couple of hours the engine burst into life and we all sat on deck basking in our success and enjoying a beer or two.

If only the governments of the world could cooperate in a similar fashion.

We'd been in Baiona nearly a week and Clive was itching to get going again. Then one morning, he noticed the local fishing fleet heading out and decided it was time to leave.

I seem to recall that we'd spent the previous evening aboard another boat consuming rum and whisky. It has to be said I wasn't feeling 100%.

So I wasn't wildly enthusiastic when Clive shook me awake and said we were heading out.

There wasn't much to do. 'Abraxis' had been ready for days.

So after a hastily gulped cup of coffee the mooring lines were untied and we started motoring out into the bay. As usual I busied myself stowing fenders and coiling mooring lines while at the same time looking around at the view.

As we cleared the harbour and headed out towards the open sea I looked ahead at a couple of the fishing boats that had departed just ahead of us . These boats were a similar size to 'Abraxis', about 35-40ft. As I watched I noticed one of them starting to lift to the swells. The bow came up and up and the boat started to rise, and she just kept rising.

At the same time, I saw the hull of another boat further ahead disappear from view until only the tips of her masts were visible. By this time, the nearer boat was high up on top of the swell and had started to fall down the other side.

Clive had seen what I'd seen and he had a huge grin on his face "Get ready for a ride" he shouted. He'd expected this.

There's nothing between the West coast of Spain and the East coast of America except for thousands and thousands of miles of open ocean.

Strong West winds like those we'd been sheltering from generate massive swells in the Atlantic . As they reach the shallower water near the coast they build into huge waves. Particularly as they funnel into the Spanish Rias cut deep into the cliffs.

He'd forgotten to mention this to me and I was frightened.

Given that the masts of these fishing boats would all but disappear in the troughs of the swells they must have been 25-30 feet high. There was little wind and the tops of the waves were smooth. They came through in a regular pattern at a frequency that was probably about twice their height.

As we entered the area where they were at their peak I hung onto the cockpit guardrail and watched with awe. There was no danger, the locals were used to them and we did just as they did, we kept to the middle of the channel and motored straight into them.

As Clive had warned, it was indeed a ride. Unsurprisingly the coffee I'd drunk earlier soon ended up over the side.

After a week ashore this was straight back to sea with a vengeance.

I guess the discomfort only lasted 15 or 20 minutes though. As we got into deeper water the swells gradually transformed into the longer lower sort typical of ocean sailing. The sort I was going to get used to over the next week.

The passage to Tenerife went well apart from one incident I'll come to in a moment. We soon fell back into our watchkeeping routine and by now we'd got well used to the way 'Abraxis' handled.

The weather was much warmer and the winds stayed generally favourable.

We had a fantastic night sailing in F6-7 and pushed 'Abraxis' to see what she could do. We stormed along at 7-9 knots all night, it was easier to do at night, we couldn't see the bend in the masts. In daylight, we'd probably have reefed sooner.

There were periods of calm as well though and as we'd already lost a week in Baiona Clive never wasted any time putting the engine on when the wind died.

It was during one of these motoring sessions that the second near disaster of the trip occurred.

It was somewhere around lunchtime, the sea was glassy, the sun was shining. We were both in the cockpit, shirts off, shorts on, and just thinking about knocking up something to eat.

I happened to glance down the companionway and to my horror saw what I thought was smoke beginning to swirl out through the hatch.

At the same time, Clive and I caught a strong smell of burning plastic and within seconds there was thick black smoke pouring out of the main cabin.

Clive dived for the engine controls to kill the motor and yelled, "Get the master switch". I was ahead of him. I'd spent enough time around vehicle electrics to have experienced a wiring fire before and the smell told me instantly that's what it was.

Every rally car has a battery master switch located in a prominent position so that in the event of a fire marshals can isolate the battery. Boats are the same, the switch on 'Abraxis' was in the engine compartment just behind the companionway ladder.

Without thinking, I took a deep breath and dived down into the smoke to get to it. I couldn't see my hand in front of my face and the acrid smoke burnt my nostrils. There were no visible flames and no heat, it just confirmed what I'd suspected, this was electrical.

It was now that all the time I'd spent working on 'Abraxis' paid off. I didn't need to see where I was going

I pulled away the ladder, wrenched open the engine compartment door and went straight to the port side bulkhead. I knew that's where the big round battery isolated switch was mounted.

My fingers touched soft warm plastic and for a few seconds I feared it was too late and that the switch wouldn't turn. Luckily it did.

Next I grabbed the bulkhead mounted fire extinguisher and gave it a blast in the direction of the switch. Then reached up above me to pull myself up into the cockpit.

Clive's big hands were there to help and I lay on the cockpit seat gulping in fresh air. Clive went along the deck to open the forward hatches and to untie the liferaft in case we had to abandon ship.

Already though it seemed that the smoke was thinning and there was still no sign of any flame. We watched with growing relief as the smoke continued to thin and some 20 or 30 minutes later it had all but disappeared.

We went below to try and figure out what had happened and it didn't take me long to find the cause.

'Abraxis' had been fitted with a new engine before we took the job on, it hadn't done many hours of running before we'd got on board. As I traced the main cable from the starter back towards the battery bank I spotted the problem. The cable had been routed through one of the hefty steel brackets of an engine mounting. The charred paint and metal spatter told me all I needed to know.

When the engine was running this cable had been rubbing against the edge of this metal bracket. This bracket was earthed to the negative side of the battery. It had taken many hours of running but eventually the thick plastic insulation layer of the cable had rubbed through.

This caused a major short circuit between the negative and positive sides of the battery. That now destroyed cut-out switch had saved us from disaster.

It took days to get the acrid plastic smell out of the boat and out of our nostrils.

We'd lost most of the engine wiring and I spent hours salvaging what I could. It took some time, but I managed to rewire the starter and charging circuits so that we could get the engine running. After that, we could get the batteries charged.

It was horrible work. The engine compartment was hot and cramped. Without wind and without power the boat rolled violently. Every so often I'd have to interrupt my work and rush up on deck to be seasick, but eventually it was done.

Clive hit the starter and we were on our way again.

In the days afterwards I came to realise that this incident had changed both of us.

I'd gained a huge boost to my confidence and Clive now realised that I could be more than just a paid hand.

When we'd come close to disaster before I was just a passenger, there was nothing I could do to help, Clive probably wished I'd not been there to witness his error.

This time it was different, I'd acted immediately. I'd done exactly the right thing and I'd then been able to use my knowledge and skills to do the repairs and get us sailing again.

Clive was no mechanic. Maybe he'd have been able to cobble something together but his large size would have made it impossible for him to get to everything.

I was pleased that I'd proved myself of value. if I'd not been there Clive would have been in real trouble. If Clive hadn't been there so would I.

He was still the skipper but now I was more than just crew, I was a proper mate in both senses of the word.

The rest of the passage went well, the sailing was relaxed and we made good progress.

This was the first time I'd experienced proper ocean sailing when the weather was mild. Biscay had been an altogether different kettle of fish and although I'd relished the challenge this was more like it.

We saw no other vessels except for some distant lights one night. There was only the sea and the sky to entertain us and they put on a superb show.

I loved the night watches, I'd never seen the stars so bright or so numerous. 'Abraxis' sailed under an incredible canopy of twinkling lights I never tired of looking at.

We saw dolphins several times and although they mainly kept clear we did have several playing in the bow wave for 10 minutes or so, magical.

Clive was as relaxed as I'd seen him in a long while. We were now back on schedule. We had only 48 hours or so of easy sailing to reach Tenerife and there was no reason to think we'd have any more problems.

So it proved, and the following day we started to pick up the first signs that our destination was drawing near.

We saw a few small birds flying around and we spotted the odd bit of foliage, a leaf or a twig, floating past the hull.

But the thing I remember most was the smell. I've already mentioned its effect when on shore but this was the first time I'd experienced something I'd read about many times.

After a long period at sea, sailors smell the land before they see it. Well at least if the winds in the right direction they do. And as all sailors know it usually does blow straight from the destination you're trying to reach. Anyway, it was early evening when I first caught the scent, a strange mix, warm and musky but distinct from the fresh ozone laden smell of the sea.

The following morning we could see the highest point on Tenerife, Mt Teide. It loomed up over the horizon through the haze and by evening we were moored stern to in the large harbour of Santa Cruz.

Santa Cruz was quite a shock to the system, after the weeks at sea Santa Cruz seemed to be a 24/7 hive of activity. Cargo ships, ferries, fishing boats and many yachts occupied the harbour which was protected by a long stone jetty.

We were tucked up well inside tied to the quay. It was crowded and it was my first experience of stern to mooring. This involves dropping the anchor and then motoring astern into any space you can find.

Inevitably this can lead to problems particularly, as was the case in Santa Cruz, when the quay is busy. We managed to moor up OK but the following day a large aluminium ketch flying the Blue Ensign managed to drop their anchor right on top of ours.

They did this despite the fact that Clive had stood on 'Abraxis's bow and pointed out in no uncertain terms where our anchor lay. To be fair, once alongside the skipper came aboard to apologise. He said that they had full scuba kit on board and that his son would dive down in the morning to sort things out. He also invited us aboard that evening for G&T's.

We accepted and had a very enjoyable evening aboard what was probably the most expensive and beautifully fitted out yacht I'd ever set foot on.

Now it should be explained that Clive and I were never going to be highly ranked for our sartorial elegance. Indeed our concession to decency that evening was to add clean T-Shirts to our shorts and flip-flops.

We hadn't seen much of our new friends since they'd arrived other than when the skipper had enquired as to the location of the 'Yacht Club'. It appeared there were three people aboard, the skipper, his son and his daughter, both in their early twenties.

As we hailed them that evening the skipper appeared up the companionway and I had to bite my lip to prevent a giggle. The only time I'd seen someone dressed in the same way was in a book about the J-class racing yachts of the 20's and 30's.

White deck shoes. White flannel trousers. Blue blazer with the Royal Cowes Yacht club emblem on the breast pocket, cravat and white skippers hat complete with gold braid. The full monty.

I nearly lost it completely when the son and daughter appeared dressed exactly the same, apart from the skippers hat.

The gin and tonics flowed. Glasses chinking with great chunks of ice from the onboard ice maker behind the oak and leather bar and the conversation flowed just as well.

After a while, Clive asked where the skipper's wife was as he'd mentioned her several times during the conversation.

"Ah", he said, "it's rather sad, we lawst her in Gib". My first thought was that he seemed to be taking her loss extremely well. But as the thought passed through my mind his son jumped in and explained.

What his father meant was that she'd taken a tumble down a flight of steps and broken her leg so they'd 'shipped her back to 'Blighty' until she recovered. "With a bit of luck she'll catch up with us in the Windies," her apparently unconcerned husband said.

It transpired that they were setting off on a 2-year circumnavigation. His good lady's misfortune wasn't going to interfere with their schedule obviously.

We also discovered that the skipper was actually quite a well-known author of pilot books. Particularly for the Scandinavian regions, indeed Clive had used a couple of his publications on delivery trips. He was interested in 'Abraxis' and, like Clive, a hugely experienced sailor. It struck me then as it's done many times since, that the love of sailing and sailboats is a great leveller. This guy was a class or two above us socially and he was certainly way above us financially and yet it didn't matter. The sea gave us a common bond. Shared hospitality came naturally.

I remembered taking 'Mor Gwas' into Cowes and how out of place I'd felt. When I mentioned to our man that I'd passed through on the way to Falmouth he said that should I pass that way again I should go to the RCYC and mention his name. I'd be more than welcomed. I never got chance to test his word, but I'm sure it was genuinely made.

We stayed in Santa Cruz for a couple of days to rest and recuperate.

I satisfied the food cravings that had built up over the previous week for chocolate and ice cream. Funnily enough, these are two foods that I generally don't eat much. But once the thought that I fancied one popped into my head without any possibility of satisfying my appetite the desire just grew and grew.

One day we took the bus into the city of Santa Cruz. My senses were overwhelmed, the bus smelled overpoweringly of people, exhaust fumes, plastic and oil. My ears were assaulted by the throbbing of the engine, the grind of gears, the din of a dozen conversations. Traffic, car horns, sirens, footsteps, hustle and bustle. It was as if the volume had been turned up to full and I felt like putting my hands over my ears.

Some people thrive in the city, they fear wide open spaces, they fear silence. I wonder how many of them have actually experienced it though. Humans have spent far longer living in the open than they have in towns and cities. To me, it's a more natural environment and I can't survive long when I can't see the horizon. I was glad to get back aboard 'Abraxis'. The harbour might have seemed busy when we arrived but after the city it was a haven of tranquility.

Once we'd re-supplied and rested up it was time to complete the last leg of our journey. A simple day sail down the East coast of Tenerife to Los Cristianos.

It was a gorgeous day and with the wind on the beam we flew along. It had been a little grey and overcast when we left Santa Cruz. But the further South we sailed the better the weather got.

I found out afterwards that although Tenerife is quite small (approximately 700 square miles). The North and the South of the island have very different climates. This is due to Mt Teide, a dormant volcano that lies in the centre of the island.

At 3,718 m (12,198 ft) high it effectively splits the weather systems. It causes most of the rain to fall on the Northern side which is accordingly green and lush. At the same time, it shelters the Southern flank from the worst of the weather so here it is predominantly dry and far warmer.

As we sailed along the cloud lifted, the sun came out and it got hot.

We anchored just off the beach of Los Cristianos in crystal clear water. It was late afternoon, but the beach was still packed. As I was tidying up the sails, I got distracted by a bronzed angel in a tiny white bikini gliding close by on a sailboard. Her dazzling smile and cheery "Ola" nearly knocked me overboard, it seemed we'd truly sailed into paradise.

We spent a week in Los Cristianos before flying back.

Mike the owner and his wife Helen were already there when we arrived and Mike was itching to see 'Abraxis' in her new form.

I was amazed that they could be considering an Atlantic crossing with a 6-month-old baby aboard. Mike had brought a friend to crew for them, but he didn't seem to have done much sailing. Not only that but we knew from experience that it took a while to learn how to handle 'Abraxis' efficiently.

We did go out for a few short sails around the bay so we could show them the basics, but Mike was keen to get away.

He'd bought a few new toys to be fitted and there were some small maintenance jobs to be done so he asked us to stay on for a few days to help out. We didn't object.

We spent most of the mornings working on the boat but we relaxed in the afternoons.

A jug or two of Sangria on the beach became very popular, sitting in the sun watching the scenery.

Clive knew a little bar just up from the harbour where we generally ate lunch and dinner. Large quantities of tapas and fresh fish were consumed.

Mike had decided it would be a good idea for them to move on board the boat before they left so Clive and I did a swop with their hotel room.

The hotel lay just behind the beach with a sea view balcony. All in all, I couldn't quite believe I was being paid to be here.

It couldn't last forever though and all too soon it was time for us to head home.

We had an early morning flight. We should have had an early night, but let's just say we made the most of our final hours on the island, and Clive set the alarm for some ungodly hour.

I slept well but was rudely awakened by Clive shaking me vigorously yelling "shit, we've overslept come on we've got to go". I registered that it was daylight, but that was about it as I threw on some clothes, grabbed my pre-packed kit bag and ran down the hotel corridor after Clive.

Mike had left us the little Renault hire car to use telling us to return it to the airport when we left.

I was very pleased that the airport wasn't far from Los Cristianos, I'm not a good passenger and Clive wasn't the best of drivers. Even in the short distance we travelled I think he managed to break every traffic regulation on the island including illegal parking.

He actually skidded to a halt right outside the terminal building and we left the car there with the keys in the ignition. Imagine the results of that stunt if repeated today.

Anyway, we got through the gate just as it was closing and collapsed into our seats.

We never did find out if the hire company got the car back OK.

That was it. The 'Abraxis' voyage was complete, we'd survived two near disasters, but we'd delivered. It was time to go home for Christmas.

10

A New Year

I SPENT Christmas and most of January with my folks and it was February before I got back to 'Mor Gwas'.

It had been a fantastic year of adventure and experience. My self-confidence had grown and I now felt more certain of my sailing ability.

I came back to 'Mor Gwas' with a list of improvements and modifications I wanted to make. I wasted no time getting started.

Over the holidays, I'd reaffirmed my decision. I was going to take 'Mor Gwas' South across Biscay and down to Portugal. I had a clear goal, my bank balance was healthy again, and I wanted to be ready when the Spring arrived.

The major modification I wanted to make to was to add a staysail.

At some point in the past, a 3ft bowsprit had been fitted which worked quite well. But I wasn't completely happy with the roller jib. It'd jammed on me in the past and even when it was working it wasn't ideal. In common with all roller jibs, it didn't reef well. This was because as it rolled up, the reduced sail area gradually climbed the forestay. This resulted in a poorly-set inefficient sail.

I'd decided to fit a baby stay and have a far smaller storm jib made that could be hanked on. Simpler and far more efficient.

I also wanted to improve the anchoring set-up by adding a larger Danforth type anchor, 20m of chain and 100m of warp.

I bought a trailing Walker log like the one we'd used on 'Abraxis' but with remote readout.

I also started looking at electronic autopilots. My wind vane worked well. But my experience on 'Abraxis' had shown me the difference a reliable autopilot would make to my single-handed sailing. In anticipation of the extra battery power it would need I upgraded the onboard 12-volt battery and fitted an LVM wind generator. Ultimately I never fitted an autopilot, the funds wouldn't stretch.

I was able to add a proper cockpit spray hood with big windows and the side dodgers I'd wanted.

By the time I'd finished, 'Mor Gwas' was starting to look like a proper cruising boat albeit a scaled down one.

It was quite tough living and working aboard during February and March. Winter that year was harsh even for Cornwall. Freezing temperatures, frequent gales and a few days of snow.

I moved the boat around quite a bit depending on the weather and my mood. I spent time tucked up a lovely little sheltered creek near Mylor Bridge. I moored to the pontoons at Mylor Yacht Harbour. And sometimes alongside the pontoon at The Pandora Inn, Restronguet.

The latter was the most enjoyable spot if not the most productive. The inland side of the pontoon was sheltered. It dried out at low water so was comfortable in all but the worst weather. I could walk ashore and there were toilets and showers available at the pub. Many a cold winter evening was spent supping a pint of HSD by the roaring log fire in the bar.

HSD, by the way, stands for Hicks Special Draught and it's a mean brew. Not for nothing do the locals call it High-Speed Diesel.

Dave had bought 'Sea Elf' round to the Pandora before I'd returned and was by now well in with the landlord and the locals.

I envied his talent of being able to talk to anyone about anything. It seemed his friendly cheerful nature always reaped rewards. In the time I knew him he was never without a lady friend whose 'hospitality' was available to him anytime he wanted it. Others gave him a hard dinghy, an outboard engine, free use of moorings in Falmouth and St Mawes and many pints of beer.

I benefited as well when he was offered various odd and sods of work. We did some decorating at a house not far up the creek from The Pandora. We did cellar work at the pub, and as Spring drew closer we helped scrub a few boats on the shingle beach nearby. It was a good way to spend the Winter, but it wasn't helping me do the work on 'Mor Gwas'.

So as April approached I retreated back to Penryn where I was closer to everything. And far less distracted.

It wasn't as quiet as I expected. 'Mor Gwas'' reappearance sparked interest from many of the other beach residents. I'd quite often spend time chatting, drinking coffee and even eating aboard other boats.

I got particularly friendly with Peter and his wife aboard a 50ft Ferro-cement ketch called 'Domboshawa'. Peter was a South African and had sailed 'Domboshawa' from Cape Town to the Med and then onwards to the UK. I'd spent 18 months working in South Africa when I left the Navy so that set us off on the right foot.

I helped with a few jobs and was rewarded with food, drink and some good company in the evenings.

The weeks spent working on 'Abraxis' had allowed me to get to know quite a few of the local tradesman as well. Colin and Dave at Spargo Sailmakers, Gerry the welder, Tom the carpenter. I got lots of help from these guys now I was back and they all wanted to hear more about how the 'Abraxis' trip had gone.

It was about this time that I got to know Tim and Heather Whelan aboard 'Ika Roa'.

She was a big James Wharram designed Polynesian catamaran. I'd been blown away at my first sight of 'Ika Roa', she was like nothing I'd ever seen before. She looked so strong and seaworthy whilst at the same time so beautiful.

When Tim told me he'd built her himself I couldn't believe it.

'Ika Roa' was joined for a while by another Wharram boat called 'Imagine' owned by a guy called Steve Turner.

I couldn't have known at the time that, decades later, these two boats would be the catalyst for the life I'm living today.

I'd spoken to Clive a few times since returning and I'd done a few jobs for him.

I'd servicing his life raft and helping rebuild the rudders on his Prout catamaran. It was a quiet time of year for the yacht delivery business. But he hinted that there were a few jobs coming up and that I would definitely be needed.

I did manage to squeeze in an early season sail up to Plymouth with another mate I'd got to know at the marina.

Chris lived on a ramshackle old Falmouth Pilot boat but had dreams to move to the Med to work as a charter skipper. To that end he was taking his Yachtmaster course and needed some crew.

He'd chartered a little Jeanneau Symphonie called 'Le Booze' for the exam.

So with a second crewman Jim we sailed up to Plymouth. We moored at Saltash right under the Tamar Bridges.

The following day we did our best to help him impress the examiner. We picked up moorings under sail. Recovered 'men overboard'. Anchored, and generally ran through all the scenarios the examiner fancied testing him on.

He even grabbed the tiller and told Chris he'd lost the steering.

This resulted in a hilarious (for us) twenty minutes trying to steer the boat with buckets trailed on warps off each quarter. It didn't work.

Anyway, Chris passed and that evening we celebrated with quite a few pints. It was a groggy sail back to Falmouth the next day.

12th March came around and I realised that it had been exactly a year since I'd first sailed 'Mor Gwas' out of Portsmouth harbour and into The Solent. Back then I'd been a complete novice, making it up as I went along. Sailing on a wing and a prayer. Wondering what I was letting myself in for, full of doubts and with no idea where my boat was taking me.

Never in my wildest dreams could I have imagined the place I now found myself. Falmouth now felt like home. I had many new friends. I'd sailed thousands of miles on many different boats. I'd found paid work doing something I loved and I was living on my own boat planning more adventure.

It hadn't been easy but then I hadn't expected it to be. The point was I was happier than I'd ever been and excited about the future. Life was good.

Late in March Clive confirmed we had another job. The boat was called 'Mr Chips' and she was a 55ft Grand Banks motor cruiser. She was currently in a small marina in Santa Ponsa Majorca. The owner, a London-based Metal Dealer (scrappy) wanted her moved to a new up-market marina in Cap Ferrat in the South of France.

A few days later Clive came down to the boat with plane and train tickets for me. He was heading out the week before as he had other business to sort out beforehand. I was to meet up with the owner's father in law Percy at Gatwick airport and we'd fly out together. After Clive left I sat down in the cockpit with a big grin on my face.

I couldn't believe it, Majorca, a big motor cruiser, The South of France, and I was being paid as well. Life was just getting better.

11

Mr Chips

THE FOLLOWING WEEK I found myself in the departure lounge at Gatwick airport scouting around for Percy.

Clive had told me to look out for an elderly gentleman with a limp which wasn't a great deal of help. It's amazing how many elderly gentlemen with a limp were wandering around the lounge that morning.

As it happened I didn't need to try too hard as Percy found me. He said I'd been easy to spot because I looked like a sailor. I suppose I hadn't realised how much I'd changed during the year I'd been on board 'Mor Gwas. Almost constant outdoor living. Sun rain and wind on the face. Fresh air in the lungs, and plenty of exercise had given me a far healthier look than the majority of landlubbers. The shorts and flip-flops in March may have given him a clue as well.

Either way I was chuffed I now looked the part.

We didn't get much chance to chat before the flight was called and Percy was sat in a different part of the plane on the way over. It'd been a long train journey from Cornwall so I did what I usually do on aeroplanes, I slept.

Once we arrived at Palma airport we hooked up again and got a taxi down to the marina at Santa Ponsa.

We soon found 'Mr Chips', she looked impressive.

The Grand Banks is a traditional boat built along the lines of a motor trawler. Very seaworthy, very capable, not so much of a floating gin palace as some of the other boats moored alongside her. But my first thought upon seeing her was that she looked a bit tired, a bit neglected.

Visit any marina anywhere in the world and the chances are you'll see more than a few boats like this. Beautiful, capable, but somehow sad. Boats are meant for the sea, they're meant to be used and far too many of them end up as occasional play things.

Percy told me later that she'd been in Santa Ponsa for about three years but that his son in law had been on board only rarely. When he did visit he'd just sit on her in the marina. Or at the most motor out into the bay where he'd anchor for an hour before heading back. So she'd sat here, forgotten most of the time.

As we climbed aboard Clive appeared from below. While he got the kettle on and started chatting to Percy I had a good look round the boat.

There was a huge saloon area aft with sliding patio doors leading out onto the sun deck. Forward, the saloon led into an open plan galley and dining area. A set of steps and a small corridor then took you to the skippers cabin abaft the bridge. The bridge itself was huge. Doors either side led to small flying wings. There was a plush helmsman's seat and plenty of seating and room for everyone. In front of the helmsman's seat was a long flat dashboard covered in dials and switches. The boat was steered with a small wooden wheel.

From the inboard bridge, another set of steps led up to the flying bridge. This was an outside steering position with duplicated controls, another plush helmsman's seat and a curved settee for passengers. It seemed very high above the deck. But I could see that it would be ideal when manoeuvring the boat as you could see all four corners with ease.

To starboard, there was a spiral staircase leading below. There I found an en-suite master cabin forward and two double cabins aft. Also a sizeable shower and heads compartment.

The engine room was accessed from a hatch on the aft deck. Although cramped there was at least enough room to get to everything. Far more than on any sailboat I'd been aboard. I had cause to be grateful for this later in the afternoon as I struggled to free the seacock for the engine cooling water.

To me 'Mr Chips' seemed to be the height of luxury. A proper floating house with all the luxuries. She seemed to have more in common with the land than the sea. Soft carpets, wall coverings, chrome, glass, all completely alien to me now.

Clive had been aboard since the previous day and I could tell that he wasn't happy.

Once the tea was brewed we all sat down at the huge aft deck table to chat. Clive came straight to the point. He told Percy that given the clear neglect the boat had suffered he wanted to delay departure by a couple of days. He needed time to check her over thoroughly. He also wanted to make sure the safety equipment was in good order and to generally tidy things up.

We were anticipating being at sea for something like 36 hours, but it was an open sea passage. The right preparation was still required.

I was half expecting to hear Percy protest but quite the opposite. He was in full agreement and said he'd ring his son in law straight away to tell him.

He came back not long afterwards and said it was all sorted. In fact, we were to take as long as we needed. His son in law was now worried that his boat would give a bad impression when we arrived in the new flashy Cap Ferrat marina.

Apparently he'd been waiting years to get a berth there. It was costing him a fortune. Percy was discreet but made it obvious he wasn't particularly impressed by his son in laws tendency to show off.

In his opinion 'Mr Chips' and Cap Ferrat were all about vanity.

That said it was his son in laws money and if that's how he wanted to spend it then so be it.

Now as it happened I knew that Clive had no more jobs on the books after this one. But he was a canny Northerner. He told Percy that staying on beyond the anticipated delivery period meant he'd have to rearrange his other jobs. I wasn't privy to the financial negotiations that followed, but I'm pretty certain he made sure he was well rewarded.

None of this mattered to me of course, I'd happily have been there for free.

I found myself grinning as I sat on this big motor cruiser in the Mediterranean sunshine. Being paid to do some far from stressful painting and varnishing for a few days, before taking a little jolly to the French Riviera was fine with me.

At the risk of repeating myself, life was good.

Over the coming days we did what we could above decks to smarten her up.

We discovered that despite appearances she was actually in pretty good order mechanically. The engines fired up first time (once I'd freed the seacocks) and ran sweetly when we motored out into the bay for a test run.

I have to admit that I was and still am somewhat anti-motorboat. 'Smokers' I call them, if you've watched the Kevin Costner movie 'Water World' you'll know what I mean. They're noisy, smelly and quite a few of them are smokey. I shouldn't stereotype. But from what I've seen the majority seem to take pleasure in charging about the place. Causing others to rock and roll in their wash and generally being anti-social.

I am and always will be a sailor. I love the peace and quiet. The effortless movement through the water with only the wind providing power and the only sound water rushing past the hull.

That said I have to admit that our first little jaunt out into the bay was an eye opener. Sitting up on the open flying bridge in a plush seat. Hands on two shiny chrome throttles connected to two huge diesel engines. It's quite intoxicating.

It was fun for 20 minutes or so but then the novelty wore off. I started to dislike the disconnection with the elements. It's no fun being able to ignore the wind completely and drive the boat in any direction you want.

We'd gained an extra member of crew the day before. His name was Charlie and like Percy he originated from the East End of London.

Charlie was a small wiry, weasel-like character. Surprisingly agile for his age which I would guess around mid to late sixties. He had been a long distance lorry driver all his working life. Back then they were a whole different breed to the drivers of today's super luxurious, ultra reliable juggernauts.

There were no tachographs, the lorries were brutish to drive, there was no health and safety, no mobile phones. These were the days when Motorways didn't exist and taking a load to Scotland could take a week.

A driver had to be independent and resourceful, all good attributes for a sailor as well.

We were soon to be grateful that Charlie was aboard.

As Clive and I got to know them both better they turned out to be real characters and both obviously 'Men Of The World'.

During our time together they entertained us with many tales of their escapades living and working in The East End during the 50's and early 60's. They'd had dealings with the infamous criminals the Kray twins. Clive and I reckoned there was quite a lot they weren't telling us.

I can't remember what profession Percy had been in but he'd done OK out of it. He had a house on the river Thames somewhere. It had a garden leading down to the waters edge and his own jetty where he kept his pride and joy. She was a pre-war motor cruiser. She'd seen service during the evacuation of troops from Dunkirk during the second world war.

Percy was an active member of The Association of Dunkirk Little Ships. Having retired spent a lot of time on the water. He admitted though that his sea-going experience was limited mainly to cross-channel jaunts during Dunkirk memorial events.

The East End was obviously a world apart in the 1950s. It was fascinating to hear first hand from guys who had lived through this little bit of history.

It took us 3 days to get 'Mr Chips' prepared but Clive eventually decided he was happy. With a decent weather forecast, we soon had the course plotted and the boat provisioned. On a bright calm sunny morning, we cast off and headed out into the bay.

From Santa Ponsa we turned right and headed for the island of Sa Dragonera. The island marks the South Western tip of Majorca. After that, we turned North. Up the West coast of Majorca until turning offshore and heading straight for Cap Ferrat.

Before reaching the Dragonera, we put into Port de Andratx to refuel. I don't know how many gallons went into the twin tanks. But the fuel kept flowing long enough for me to think we'd got a serious leak somewhere.

I couldn't help wondering why some folks lay out so much cash to get their boats from A to B. With a few bits of canvas and a breeze they could do it for free.

Once underway again we set our course and chugged away at a steady 8 knots. There wasn't a lot to do. Clive and Percy were on the bridge so Charlie and I sat on the aft deck with a Coke nicely chilled with ice from the onboard freezer.

Once we'd rounded Sa Dragonera the scenery became spectacular. This North West facing coast of Majorca has high cliffs rising vertically out of the sea, the sky was blue and the sun was warm, not bad at all for March.

After a few hours though I was a bit bored. The constant noise and vibration from the engines was grating. To add to the discomfort, we discovered that 'Mr Chips' rolled like a pig in the steady swell. Hardly surprising given her shallow draft and high topsides. But very different from the gentle motion of a good sailboat.

After lunch, as I was making my way up to the bridge to see if I could take a hand at the wheel the engine revs suddenly slowed.

Strange I thought, then both engines stopped.

My first thought was that maybe we'd fouled the propeller as had happened on 'Abraxis'. But there'd been no vibration or other warning and there were two separate propellers. It seemed unlikely. On top of that the engines had stopped dead.

Charlie appeared out of the saloon straight away . He got the aft deck hatch open so he could get into the engine space. We knew that his years of driving had given him a pretty good knowledge of diesel engines. So he'd been promoted to ship's engineer.

I was particularly pleased about that. Not only was my knowledge of diesel engines a bit thin. But I knew that if he hadn't been there it would have been me down in that cramped smelly engine compartment. It would have been me fighting seasickness whilst trying to sort things out.

Clive and I knew as soon as the engines stopped that we were going to be in a spot of bother unless the engines could be restarted quickly.

There was a fresh onshore breeze blowing and we were probably 3-4 miles offshore. Downwind of us there was nothing but steep rocky cliffs.

'Mr Chips' had a high freeboard. In effect a slab sided sail. Her shallow draft and lack of keel meant that there was little resistance to drifting.

We estimated that we were now moving towards the shore at 2-3 knots. That meant that in something like an hour we'd be uncomfortably close to those towering cliffs. In truth we already were.

Whilst Charlie and Percy beavered away down in the engine space Clive and I set to trying to buy us some more time.

The depth sounder showed around 500ft of water underneath us. Dropping the hook wasn't an option.

There was only one obvious thing we could do and that was to rig up some sort of sea anchor.

Luckily there were a couple of old car tyres aboard which had been used as fenders. I dug them out while Clive unshackled the bow anchor. It only took a few minutes to loop the anchor line around the tyres then secure it back on itself with the shackle and drop the tyres over the bow.

We gradually payed out the line until we had the full length of anchor rode deployed. Probably about 200 feet.

The difference was amazing.

'Mr Chips' swung her bows into the wind and seemed to be holding her own. As an added bonus, this new bows on position stopped her rolling so much. It made Charlie and Percy's work down below much more comfortable.

Once we'd done the job we headed back to the engine space to see how they were getting on.

Charlie showed us one of the filters, completely clogged with a waxy gunge. Percy said that over the past years 'Mr Chips' had never been fully fuelled. Now it seemed obvious what had happened.

The half empty tanks had accumulated crap inside them whilst the boat was moored. Then, when we fuelled the boat for the trip, it became submerged with the diesel and had softened.

Once at sea the constant rolling had gradually dislodged this residue and it began entering the fuel lines. It didn't take long for them to block completely.

Over the next thirty or forty minutes, Charlie and Percy worked heroically cleaning the filters and bleeding the fuel lines. Once they'd done that Clive hit the starter buttons and with a cloud of smoke both engines fired up.

It was a welcome relief and even the choking diesel fumes smelt good. I headed up to the bow and got the sea anchor in using the power windlass. Thanking my stars as I did so that we were on a boat with such luxuries. The thought of hauling up 200 feet of line and two car tyres manually did not appeal.

The engines continued to run but they didn't sound completely healthy. Now and again they slowed or missed a beat before picking up again.

Charlie spent most of his time in the engine compartment keeping an eye on them.

There was no way we were going to head off overnight with unreliable engines. There was some risk in closing the shore again we didn't have a choice. We needed to get things sorted properly.

According to the charts, there was only one viable harbour within 40 miles and that was Soller. Clive set a course and an hour or so later we were safely tied up alongside.

Soller turned out to be a lovely place and I think everyone was pleased we'd got to see it.

Compared to the 'Abraxis' trip things were very relaxed. Percy had basically told Clive that there was no rush to get 'Mr Chips' to Cap Ferrat. And as Clive and I were being paid for our time we happily went along.

Everyone was treating it as a holiday and even the problems we'd had seemed nothing more than exciting little adventures sent to spice up the day.

Percy was insistent that we ate and drank completely at his expense. That evening we enjoyed some of the best seafood I've ever had. We ate on a restaurant balcony overlooking the beautiful harbour. The excellent food was washed down with some very pleasant white wine. This was followed by large glasses of brandy as a nightcap.

Next morning we tracked down the local marine engine specialist. Amazingly he turned up on the pontoon within a few hours of ringing him.

He spent the next hour putting some sort of additive in the tanks. Running the engines. Cleaning the filters and then repeating the process. All the while with Charlie looking over his shoulder. Because he didn't trust 'these daygo mechanics'.

Somewhat of an Alf Garnet character was Charlie.

It took most of the day to get things sorted. Clive suggested we leave that evening but Percy said he'd far rather enjoy another night ashore and leave in the morning.

Given that he was the official representative of our client and the customer is alway right Clive was happy to go along.

Even more so because Percy insisted we join him and Charlie again and still wouldn't let us put our hands in our pockets. It was getting repetitive but once again I found myself wondering if I'd got the best job in the world.

So it was, with slightly thick heads, we set off the following morning.

The sea had flattened out a lot but none the less we had a slightly strained first few hours as we listened intently to the engines for any sign of trouble. We needn't have worried though, they ran smoothly.

To be honest, I found the voyage a bit tedious.

The engine noise was constant and although the boat was pretty well sound insulated the noise and vibration became a bit wearing.

Even in the flat waters 'Mr Chips' rolled a lot and my seasickness came on.

I'd long since learned how to deal with it. Every 30 minutes or so I'd go to the head and throw up. After a good gargle with fresh water and before the next bout of nausea, I'd keep sipping water and nibbling on dry biscuits or bread.

Percy was surprised that I treated it so lightly, but I just thought of it as a minor inconvenience. It never once stopped me functioning during any of our delivery trips.

In any case, it usually passed after the first 24 hours of a long passage. As it happened this particular trip wasn't going to take us much longer than that as we ploughed along at 10knots leaving a wide frothing wake behind us.

All in all it was pretty boring, no sails to handle, perfect weather and little to look at except the sea and the sky.

As we motored on into the night it turned really dark. There was no moon and a lot of cloud. 'Mr Chips' became somewhat akin to an ocean liner lit up like a Christmas tree.

This was something I'd never experienced on a sailboat where power always seems to be in short supply and lights are kept to a minimum.

The bridge was kitted out with red lighting so as not to interfere with night vision.

In front of the heavily padded leather helmsman's seat was a huge sloping dashboard covered in glowing dials and switches. Apart from the occasional glance at engine temperatures and compass. to check the autopilot had us on the right course. It was just a case of keeping a good lookout.

There wasn't much in the way of traffic between Majorca and The South of France at that time of year but fishing vessels were plentiful.

We were moving at faster speeds than I'd been used to and I knew that we'd be closing on any other vessels out there much more quickly as a consequence.

'Mr Chips' was equipped with a big old Decca radar set. Just to starboard of the helm there was a huge round orange screen with a black viewing tube attached.

I was sharing the watch with Percy and he absolutely loved this radar.

He glued his eyes to the viewing tube every few minutes whilst at the same time twiddling knobs left right and centre until satisfied. After which he'd say "No vessels in range Skipper".

Now it just so happened that for some 15 minutes I'd been watching a cluster of lights some distance off our port bow. We were closing on them but it looked as if we'd pass well clear.

Mediterranean fishing vessels aren't exactly renowned for using all the correct regulation navigation lights. In any case they can easily be obscured by working lights and the even bigger white lights they shine down into the water to attract fish.

But, from what I could see, there was a group of perhaps half a dozen vessels doing some sort of fishing but they weren't moving much.

Anyway, Percy had checked the radar 3 or 4 times and informed me on each occasion that there were "No vessels in range Skipper". The last time he'd done it we were within a mile of the group.

I thanked Percy for his report and then said, "Strange that Percy, I wonder what all those lights are over there then". Percy followed the direction of my gaze and blurted out "Bloody hell where did they come from". Then raced back to the radar where he again started twiddling the knobs furiously. "Well they're definitely not there Neil, I can tell you that," he said.

By this time the lights were fading away astern so I replied, "Well that's OK then Percy, we'll stay on course eh".

Radar can be a wonderful thing when the visibility goes to pot but when I can I far prefer to use the MKI eyeball.

It was about mid-morning the following day when we picked out the hazy coastline of Southern France. It's easy to spot from far out at sea because of the high cliffs and mountains that rise up immediately behind the coast.

As with our landfall in Tenerife I once again experienced the smell of land only this time I'm sure there was a hint of garlic mixed in there.

By mid afternoon we were motoring gently past Nice, onwards towards Cap Ferrat with its luxury villas, and into St Jean Marina.

The sun was hot, the sky was blue and there wasn't a breath of wind. Clive was pleased about that.

He'd been worried that the infamous Mistral wind might have blown up as it often does in the afternoons.

'Mr Chips' might have had powerful engines but, as I've already said, she was high-sided. She would be very hard to handle in the crowded confines of the marina we now found ourselves in.

The potential for expensive insurance claims around this place boggled the mind.

At 55ft overall I considered 'Mr Chips' to be a sizeable vessel. But as we gently motored past the other boats berthed there my jaw dropped further and further. Most of these vessels were motor cruisers and it seems most of them were close to 100ft long.

Many of them were bigger still, a couple even had landing pads for helicopters. They all had speedboats and jet skis aboard. I was constantly dazzled by huge areas of gleaming white fibreglass. Acres of smoked glass and endless miles of highly polished stainless steel.

'Mr Chips' looked out of place. She was too small and too shabby. But from what I could see she was still the most seaworthy looking vessel there.

Clive had been on the VHF to announce our arrival and almost immediately a fast RIB appeared on our bow to lead us to our allocated berth. Even the RIB was shiny and new. Driven by an equally shiny young lad dressed in immaculate white bell bottoms, stripy blue and white jumper and a white Breton cap. I went below to get my sunglasses as my eyes were beginning to water.

There were two other clones of the RIB driver on the pontoons waiting to take our lines. I watched with admiration as Clive skilfully reversed 'Mr Chips' into a vacant slot.

Our berth was alongside what was thankfully one of the smaller boats in there. Actually I noticed later that the boats were pretty much berthed according to size. The largest taking pride of place near the town.

Clive had seen this all before but Percy, Charlie and I were incredulous.

I guess we all know that there are places where the seriously wealthy come to play, we've all seen it on the TV. But to be there, to see it in the flesh, is just overwhelming.

That evening as we walked the marina front Boulevard I felt like an alien that had landed on another planet.

To all intents and purposes that's exactly what I was.

There were women walking along the street with handbags that likely cost more than 'Mor Gwas'. Supercars cruised up and down the road, everywhere you looked screamed 'look at how much money I have'. I was transfixed and horrified at the same time.

Percy and Charlie just stared quietly with smiles on their faces. They'd spent their lives working their way up from poor beginnings in the East End. To them this was the ultimate paradise. To them life was a game with money as the scorecard.

I hated it. This place represented everything I was trying to escape and suddenly I wanted to be back aboard 'Mor Gwas'.

We ate at an incredibly expensive restaurant that evening but I didn't really enjoy it. The food was nearly as rich as the clientele.

The following morning Clive decided we'd hop round to Beaulieu just down the coast so that we could clear Customs.

We could have taken a taxi but the boat seemed a nicer option and besides Percy had asked Clive to give him some boat handling instruction in the bay.

We had a fun few hours doing man overboard drills and opening up the throttles a bit to see what 'Mr Chips' could do.

She was certainly the fastest apartment I'd ever been on.

We moored up in Beaulieu against the quay and Clive went off to sort the Customs paperwork. When he got back we made ready to depart.

But as soon as Clive applied a bit of throttle to the starboard engine the whole boat started vibrating. He throttled back immediately and this time we knew exactly what it was, we'd got a fouled propeller.

This was getting repetitive.

So once again muggins found himself overboard with a diving knife trying to get the prop free.

From the point of view of access, things were a lot easier than the last time I'd done this on 'Abraxis'. We were in flat water and the props of 'Mr Chips' weren't as deep under water. But what I hadn't accounted for was the cold.

The water was absolutely icy, far colder than when I'd swum in

Biscay in December. I lasted only about 10 minutes. Hacking away at the old sacking that was wrapped around the prop before I had to be hauled out.

We'd gathered quite an audience but I was oblivious as, wrapped in a blanket, I tried to walk up and down the quay to warm up. It took about 15 minutes for me to stop shivering and for my hands to be steady enough to hold a mug of steaming tea.

Charlie stepped up to the plate and jumped in after me to finish the job. He was out after a few minutes and actually got a round of applause from the gathered onlookers.

I ribbed him later about snatching my glory.

By the time we'd both got dry and dressed and were ready to set off again the Mistral wind had arrived good and proper. This was what Clive had feared when we first arrived. It was blowing straight across the harbour and pushing 'Mr Chips' hard against the quay wall.

We had other boats moored fore and aft of us and there just wasn't any room to manoeuvre. Sometimes it's possible to 'warp' a boat out of these positions but there were no pontoons or quays near enough for us to get a line attached.

Clive got on the VHF to the marina control and explained that we couldn't get off the wall without help. They sent down a decent sized RIB which took a line from our bow. They then pulled it out as we pivoted 'Mr Chips' off the starboard quarter using a couple of large fenders against the wall.

Even with the RIB it was a tough manoeuvre and I was pleased to be handling ropes and fenders rather than throttles.

As soon as our bows were clear Clive had to apply power to get enough way on the boat to counteract the force of the wind.

The RIB driver had obviously done this many times before and released the line at exactly the right time so that I could pull it aboard smartly.

Once again Clive and I had shown what we could do and later on he congratulated me for the way I'd handled things.

I hadn't realised at the time but at no point had Clive had to tell me what to do or where to be. I'd understood immediately what was needed and just got on and did it.

Percy and Charlie also expressed their admiration and I confess to feeling quite proud of myself that evening.

We stayed on 'Mr Chips' for another week at St Jean, we spent the days sanding, varnishing and painting. It was enjoyable work and there was always something going on close by to keep boredom at bay.

One afternoon a couple of minivans arrived on the quay nearby and out piled a camera crew and several rather stunning looking women.

After about an hour of faffing around with cameras, tripods and lights the girls appeared out of one of the vans. To our delight they were wearing nothing but tiny bikini bottoms.

They started posing right beneath our bows.

It has to be said that work ground to a halt aboard 'Mr Chips'.

Well it did as far as Charlie and I were concerned. Clive kept painting although I did eventually suggest that he stopped as I wasn't sure the owner really wanted one of his cabin windows painted over.

Percy had been in town during this distraction, but we made sure to describe in great detail what he'd missed when he got back on board later.

In the evenings, Percy always treated us to a meal in town. Later we'd adjourn to the nearest bar where we'd pass the night away weaving stories and generally making merry.

It was fun but it had to end and as March drew to a close we flew back to Gatwick.

After a long drive back to Cornwall it was 2: 30 am before I crashed in my bunk back aboard 'Mor Gwas'.

It had been another fantastic trip. But Spring had arrived and I wanted to get back to working on my own plans and dreams rather than someone else's.

In my sleep that night I saw 'Mor Gwas' sailing the same blue Mediterranean waters I'd just left.

I couldn't wait.

12

Preparing For Sea

THE WEATHER in early April was typical for the UK. We had spells of heavy rain and strong winds interspersed with some decent sunny ones.

It seemed an eternity since I'd sailed 'Mor Gwas'. I took every opportunity to get out when I could.

My confidence had grown. Even when it was blowing I was happy to sail around in the comparative shelter of the Carrick Roads. I was learning better how 'Mor Gwas' handled when she was reefed down and experimenting with my new storm jib.

I spent a lot of time moored up at The Pandora and Mylor and quite often I'd sail in company with Dave on 'Sea Elf'.

We sailed across to the Helford. Spent a few days exploring beautiful little places like Gillan Creek and the river up to Gweek.

We explored The Percuil river past St Mawes. Right the way up The Fal into the Truro river and up to the city of Truro itself.

Dave and I had become good friends. We had a common bond in that we both lived on tiny boats. We had very similar philosophies. Taking things as they came and trying to get as much enjoyment out of life as we could.

Dave always had me beat on attitude though.

I was and still am, prone to depression. Particularly when the weather is bad. My mood seems to decline in direct relation to the amount of time the sunshine has been absent.

With Dave though it was different. I never once saw him react badly to anything.

One day when we were both out sailing in gusty winds, the mast on 'Sea Elf' broke just above the crosstrees. I'd have been gutted. He just laughed.

He always had that damn big smile on his face. He always went out of his way to try and cheer folks up if he thought they were down. He was good for me to be around.

We had many memorable days, but one incident in particular sticks in my mind.

After a great days sailing, we decided to explore the little inlet of St Just in Roseland.

There's really not a lot to it, but it's a truly magical place.

There's a small boat yard just inside the creek. Then, after following a dog leg around a sand spit where boats can be laid up. You can get into a shallow drying pool directly in front of the Church.

It's here that the word magical fits best, the Church at St Just in Roseland is like no other.

It's completely sheltered from most winds. The graveyard surrounding the Church on three sides is terraced and wooded. The vegetation is almost sub-tropical.

The whole place feels like it's been transported from another country.

It's unlike any other English Church I know.

We decided that the pool would be an excellent place to spend the night.

The Hurley Silhouette is quite shallow draft (less than 3ft) and has bilge keels. This meant that 'Mor Gwas' and 'Sea Elf' could creep into places out of reach of most sailboats. Once there we could then take the ground quite happily when the tide went out.

So we gently motored the boats round the spit and into the

pool. We dropped our anchors in the middle, went astern and dropped anchors near the bank. Then, after bedding them in, adjusted the lines so that the boats sat nicely alongside each other. Facing the church.

It was idyllic, the birdsong as the sun went down was replaced by the hoots of owls.

There wasn't a breath of wind and as we sat in the cockpit with steaming cups of rum laced coffee both Dave and I fell silent.

Just taking in the surreal atmosphere of it all.

After a few minutes, Dave said, "do you believe in ghosts?"

Given our location overlooking dozens of ivy-covered gravestones I suppose it was a good question to ask.

"Yep," I answered, "I reckon there are too many stories about them for there not to be something in it".

Strangely, just at that moment, a chilly breeze sprang up from nowhere.

Despite our sheltered position, the wind shook the branches of the trees behind the church. Then it seemed to blow down across the water until it passed right over us and disappeared leaving all as calm as before it arrived.

Dave and I looked at each other and grinned but just as we did so the peace and quiet was shattered by the most blood-curdling scream.

My heart jumped into my throat, we both jolted upright, neither of us having the first clue as to what we'd just heard.

At that point, Heidi, Dave's little Jack Russell Terrier, came leaping up out of the cabin with a can of dog food apparently glued to her nose.

In an instant Dave realised what had happened. He was in the habit of feeding Heidi just half a can of food at a time. Afterwards he'd just push the three-quarter opened lid back into the top of the tin until the next feeding time.

Heidi had somehow managed to dislodge the tin from where it was stowed. Then she'd stuck her tongue into it to get at the meat.

Obviously this had pushed the lid further into the tin which was fine. But then when she'd come to pull her tongue out, it had also pulled the lid back on its 'hinge'.

It had trapped her tongue between the outside of the can and the sharp serrated edge of the lid.

Unsurprisingly this had caused some pain hence the yelp. But with her snout buried in the can and her tongue wedged tight, this yelp had been transformed into the scream Dave and I heard.

It took Dave only a minute to get her free and a brief inspection showed no damage had been done. At least not to Heidi. It's a wonder Dave and I didn't have some sort of cardiac arrest though.

We subsequently ditched the coffee and just drank the rum.

All of these little adventures were great fun, but I'd fallen into a bit of a trap.

I was enjoying myself to the detriment of getting the remaining large jobs done on 'Mor Gwas'. I had two particular ones on the list and over the following weeks I knuckled down and got them sorted.

First I designed and had made a substantial mounting bracket and pole for the LVM wind generator. There was a blacksmith in Commercial Road Penryn who helped enormously with that.

Then I completely re-built the wind vane self-steering following a design I found in a book from the library.

It ended up being made from scrap plywood that I got for nothing and various screws and bolts from Trago Mills. Key to the whole thing though was a big ball race bearing acquired for the princely sum of £2 from the local garage.

With these two bits of kit hanging off the stern 'Mor Gwas' really started to stand out as something different.

I'd been sailing a bit of a stealth boat up to that point. To the casual observer, she was just a run of the mill day sailer, pretty, but not something you'd really go to sea in. But with these bits of kit I was signalling two things.

First the wind generator told folks that I spent a lot of time aboard and needed plenty of power.

Second the self-steering, well that probably caused a bit more puzzlement. Surely you'd only need that for long distance sailing so what was one doing on that little 18 footer? Surely he can't need it, surely he can't sail across oceans?

Well as I sailed around The Carrick Roads there must have been a few people wondering. But none of them could have guessed my plans and many of them wouldn't have believed me even if I'd told them.

To be honest, it was only now that I'd started to believe it myself.

Months of vague thought. Occasional comments about sailing South sometime. They'd now turned into something far more definite.

After my trips on 'Abraxis' and 'Mr Chips' I knew clearly what I wanted next. I wanted to sail across the Bay of Biscay. I wanted to explore the coasts of Spain and Portugal. I wanted to sail 'Mor Gwas' through the Straits of Gibraltar and into The Mediterranean. I wanted to escape the rain and the cold and follow the sun, and I'd be doing it soon.

Towards the end of May 'Mor Gwas' was as ready as I could make her.

I'd sailed her in winds up to F7 and in some pretty choppy seas in the Bay. I'd got the self-steering working well. I'd dried her out on the shingle beach near the Pandora and got a new coat of antifoul paint slapped on. My new cutter rig was sorted and with the baby stay fitted I could now sail with a storm jib.

I'd got over 100 cans of tinned food and some 18 gallons of fresh water aboard and all my paperwork was in order. All I needed now was the right weather.

On 20th May, I moved 'Mor Gwas' down from Penryn for the last time. I'd come to think of Church Beach as home. It felt strange untying my bow lines from the trees, digging out my stern anchors and heading downriver.

The only evidence of my time there was the little stone causeway which now looked natural. Covered as it was in mud and weed.

I hoped the next resident would appreciate it.

I picked up a mooring off The Greenbank Hotel and spent a few hours washing mud off everything. Mud was the one thing about Penryn I wasn't going to miss.

Once everything was clean I sailed round to The Pandora to say goodbye to Dave and the gang. As a result I very nearly ended up with a hole in my boat.

As I approached the Pandora pontoon, sailing quite fast, 'Mor Gwas' suddenly slowed and veered round to starboard. I had no idea what had happened until I looked down by the stern and saw a rope wrapped around the rudder skeg.

At the same instant I saw the outline of a small motor cruiser just under the water, I'd missed the coachroof by inches.

Once safely moored up I found out from Dave that the cruiser had sunk on its mooring just an hour before I arrived. Salvage divers were en route from Falmouth to try and lift her.

I'd had a lucky escape. Who knows what damage I might have done hitting her at 5 knots.

The following day was one of torrential rain and NW 7-8 winds and I spent most of it inside the Pandora. The forecast said that the wind would stay in from the North for the following week but that it would continue to moderate. The direction was right, it was just a case of waiting.

On Thursday 24th, it had eased a little and backed slightly to the East and I sailed back into Falmouth.

I picked up a mooring close to Peter and Isabel on 'Domboshawa' and that evening sat aboard with them talking through the weather.

The low in Biscay was moving away SE and the low over Germany was doing the same. The 17: 55 forecast for sea area Plymouth predicted NW 4-5 decreasing 3-4, Peter agreed that things looked good for departure.

It was good to get my thoughts confirmed by someone else.

But by 11 pm that night 'Mor Gwas' was rocking and rolling on her mooring with the wind gusting a good 7.

Not only that but it was foggy.

The midnight shipping forecast said the same as before.

I just didn't know what to think.

I eventually dozed off with my mind drifted this way and that, I'd just have to see what the morning would bring.

13

Departure (Friday)

I WOKE AT 6: 30 to a different day.

The skies had cleared, the breeze was down to a gentle force 3. It was time to go.

After all frustration and waiting, all the nervousness disappeared. I felt elated and eager to move, so after a quick cup of coffee I slipped the mooring and motored out into the Roads.

There was no one awake on 'Domboshawa', the harbour was quiet. There was no one there to wave me off, no one there to share the moment with.

Any early morning strollers would just think I was out to make the most of a days sailing. They would never have guessed that my next intended port of call was Baiona in Northern Spain. I could hardly believe it myself as I unlashed the ties and hoisted sail.

Pendennis Castle. St Mawes Castle. St Anthony lighthouse and Black Rock all slid slowly astern. Falmouth had become my home. But now it was time to explore over that horizon.

I found myself grinning as I shouted "Bye Bye Falmouth".

An hour and a half of gentle sailing saw me round the Manacles, and I was able to put the boat on a heading of 215 degrees - South West. This was the course I intended to follow right into the Bay of Biscay.

Although it put me further out to sea than was necessary, it meant I would be well clear of the main shipping lanes. Close proximity to thousands of tons of steel moving at 20 knots is not desirable when sailing a small fibreglass boat.

During one tense night watch off Ushant a few months before I'd had twenty sets of lights in view at one time. They were all moving in different directions and twice we'd had to alter course to get out of harms way.

That had been on 'Abraxis'. A thirty footer with a big engine. I had no desire to repeat the experience on 'Mor Gwas' with her little Suzuki outboard.

Giving land a wide berth also meant that I would have more sea-room in the event of any nasty weather blowing up.

I was confident in the boats ability to ride out a gale. But with a small boat you must reef, slow down and heave-to much earlier than a larger boat. So you need more room. I had cause to be thankful for this planning later.

The change of course had put the wind onto the starboard quarter and she was flying along at 4 knots. Her top speed was about 5.5 knots so that was pretty good.

I was well pleased with the way things were going and I didn't even mind the steady drizzle which was now falling.

I steered by hand for most of the morning as I wanted to keep an accurate course. I also needed to keep a good look-out for the shipping I knew I would find off The Lizard.

This was something I couldn't avoid. The Lizard is one of the main turning points for ships heading up and down The Channel. I knew from experience how busy it could be.

In the event I only saw three ships but one came close enough for me to alter course to avoid crossing her bow.

A couple of miles clear of The Lizard the wind picked up to a force 4-5 and backed round to the West a little. This put the boat onto more of a reach. My speed picked up to 4.5-5 knots and, now I was in the open sea, the waves seemed enormous.

After weeks of inshore sailing around the sheltered waters of Falmouth I'd forgotten what proper sea looked like. I soon got used to it though and started to enjoy the exciting sailing.

It was exhilarating and 'Mor Gwas' was performing brilliantly. Riding over the waves like an ocean racer. After a few hours of fun, I connected up my wind vane self-steering.

As already mentioned, It was a very simple. Just a vertically pivoted vane connected directly to the tiller with cord and pulleys and balanced with shock cord. I'd tried it in many different wind strengths and conditions and found it worked quite well. The secret was to trim the sails properly so that it had to do as little work as possible.

Obviously it wouldn't steer as well as an electronic autopilot but at least it would give me a rest now and then.

I love the sensation of being alone on a boat that's sailing herself. It's difficult to describe the feeling when you go up to the pulpit and look back to the empty cockpit and the empty sea beyond the wake.

It's as if the boat is saying, 'It's OK, I'm in control, just enjoy yourself'. So that's just what I did.

I knocked up a ham sandwich and a mug of tea, checked my navigation and generally tried to settle down to life at sea. The wind seemed to have freshened a bit so with the approach of night I took a couple of reefs in the main to slow down. After all I wasn't in any hurry.

I don't think I thought about at the time, but I didn't have anything else to eat that day. Mainly because my appetite had gone. Something which is quite normal for me in the first 24 hours or so at sea.

It got dark about 2300 and I put the masthead light on. I steered for most of the night, it was uneventful apart from one very strange experience.

At some point in the early hours I started hearing a weird kind of buzzing noise. It was faint and high pitched. At first I thought it must be tinnitus brought on by tiredness. But the noise kept getting louder until I could pinpoint it to somewhere off the port bow.

It was a dark night and I strained my eyes in the direction of the noise. All the while trying to figure out what the hell it could be.

As I stared into the darkness I started to make out a black rectangular shadow with a white line at the bottom edge.

It was moving fast at 90 degrees to 'Mor Gwas' some distance off and crossing in front of us.

As the distance got less I realised that the white line I could see was water being pushed along.

It suddenly dawned on me what I was looking at.

It was a submarine conning tower.

She was showing no lights and running fast just under the surface.

Within minutes she'd passed ahead and disappeared into the darkness. As my heart rate started to come down I wondered if she even knew I was there.

After that I did try sleeping a couple of times but I couldn't relax.

That close encounter left me worried about what other hazards might be around.

14

Day 1 (Saturday)

DAWN CAME AT ABOUT 0500.

I was feeling a little tired but not too bad.

The isolation was beginning to make itself felt though.

All around me was grey, no ships, a few birds, other than that it was just me and my boat.

Uncannily, just as these thoughts were passing through my head, 'Mor Gwas' was suddenly surrounded by a school of porpoises.

They stayed a while, leaping out of the water and playing in the bow wave. All my negative thoughts vanished in an instant as I watched their joyful display.

It's something I've noticed during my time at sea. Cetaceans have this seemingly psychic ability to appear just when us humans are beginning to feel down and fearful. It's as if they pick up on the thoughts and come along to help.

Maybe one day we'll find out that these creatures are far more intelligent than we are.

Unfortunately, the morning shipping forecast soon dampened my newly buoyed mood.

The synopsis wasn't good and gave the first clue that things were going to get nasty. I

t began to look like a repeat performance of the scenario played out a few days before.

The low over Europe wasn't filling, it was deepening. It was also moving South West, back towards us, a bit further away than the last one, but still too close for comfort.

The forecast predicted NW 5-6 occasionally 7 for Plymouth and Biscay.

There was nothing I could do about it. The Walker log, which I'd been trailing astern since The Manacles showed we'd covered the best part of 60 miles.

I was quite happy with our progress. I reckoned that if the low continued to track as before we'd probably have the worst of it to the North of us.

I could only hope. With daylight, I was able to relax a bit more.

I hove-to briefly for some toast and marmalade and a coffee. After checking there were no ships on the horizon anywhere I put the self-steering to work and slept for about an hour. It was my first since leaving Falmouth.

As I came round from my nap I realised that there was a bit more wind noise and motion.

Up in the cockpit, I found that the wind and seas had increased a lot in the short time I'd been below.

The wind had veered as well putting 'Mor Gwas' off course by about 20 degrees. Wind vane self-steering holds the boat at a set angle to the wind, so if the wind changes direction so does the boat.

I decided to make things a bit more comfortable.

I rolled up the foresail and double reefed the main. But even with this small sail area 'Mor Gwas' was still doing 4 knots.

Although the seas were quite big she rode them well. Only occasionally did a 'sloppy' wave come over the dodgers into the cockpit. But it was nothing that the drains couldn't easily cope with.

We carried on like this for about an hour. But I began noticing that more waves were slopping over into the cockpit. Not only that but heavier ones were starting to slam into the hull.

Things were getting very uncomfortable. I decided to heave-to and rest for a bit, 'Mor Gwas' and I weren't up for this kind of sailing.

Once I'd stopped the boat things got a bit quieter and I went below to make a brew. The motion of the past few hours was starting to affect me though, so the tea and biscuits didn't stay down long.

I've mentioned before that sea-sickness has plagued me ever since I started sailing. So I wasn't too worried about it now. I'd actually been expecting it. I knew I'd have to keep hydrated though so I filled a bottle with water I could sip.

An hour later it was obvious that the wind had increased yet further. Every so often 'Mor Gwas' would be heeled over in a gust until the lee-rail went under.

I went outside with the intention of putting the last reef in the main and remaining hove-to. But by the time I'd tied the reefing pennants the wind had increased enough for me to decide to furl the sail altogether and lie a-hull.

I was cold, wet and knackered by the time I'd done the job and it took me a good while under my sleeping bag to stop shivering.

A hot drink was what I craved but it was now too rough to risk boiling the kettle and I figured it wouldn't stay down long anyway.

So I sipped some more tepid water instead, it was a poor substitute.

After drowsing for a while I woke feeling none too good.

I stuck my head out of the companionway for fresh air but not for long. The wind had started whipping spume off the tops of the waves and I couldn't leave the hatch open.

It must have been about 1000 Saturday when I started to lie a-hull and little did I know that it would be another 24 hours before I could sail again.

I spent most of that time lying on my bunk with my left shoulder wedged under the bookshelf so I didn't get thrown out. I never really slept. I just lay there listening to the noise and wondering how much more the boat could take.

Every now and then a wave would break over the cabin so all I could see out of the windows was water.

Often 'Mor Gwas' fell off the top of a wave and dropped hard into the trough behind. That was what worried me the most, it felt like we were hitting concrete, the whole boat shook and vibrated.

The seasickness had a strong hold now and I was retching into the cockpit every 30 minutes or so. Not that there was anything much to bring up as my few stomach contents had long since departed.

As I already said, I knew the dangers of dehydration and was taking sips of water afterwards. But I had begun to taste blood which only added to my anxiety.

I didn't know what else to do other than lie still and hope things settled down.

Now and again I would sit up and have a look through the windows. But I never saw anything, just grey sea, white foam and dark clouds.

The motion of the boat was beginning to wear on me, even lying on the bunk required physical effort.

My muscles tensed with each movement tiring me even more and making it impossible to relax.

Add in the psychological stress of noise and fear and you have a debilitating cocktail.

Imagine being trapped in a fibreglass box bouncing down a rocky hillside for hours on end and you'll get some idea.

I do remember losing it at one point. Mumbling repeatedly something like 'enough, please, enough'.

It didn't do any good.

15

Day 2 (Sunday)

IT WAS A LONG NIGHT. But by dawn on Sunday morning I got the impression that the wind had dropped a little.

The seas were big but seemingly easing.

I was still seasick and felt completely drained but I knew I couldn't stay in the cabin forever.

So I opened up the hatch, slid out the washboard and crawled out into the cockpit.

It was a mess.

The tail ends of sheets and halyards had come undone and were snaked around the place. There were bits of seaweed wrapped around the shroud plates. Even a couple of small silver fish lying on the cockpit seats.

The wind was now dropping quite fast and although the seas were still big I needed to get the boat moving again.

So I decided to make sail. It was shocking how weak I felt as I went to work. Every joint and muscle in my body seemed to be aching and it took a huge effort to get the double reefed main up.

I unfurled about half of the foresail and came back onto my heading of 215 degrees. It felt a lot better to be sailing again and it helped take my mind off the way I was feeling.

But the Sunday 0625 forecast didn't give me the much-needed hope I was looking for.

The dry tones of the broadcaster came crackling over the transistor radio. "Plymouth, Biscay NW or W 6-7 occasionally gale 8". The words hit me like a punch to the kidneys.

Fear brought the bile up from my stomach and I dry retched over the cockpit side. Things were getting serious.

I had to force myself to think straight.

My instinct was to crawl back into my bunk, curl up into the foetal position and pray for deliverance.

But I've never been religious and cold logic told me I was going to have to find my own way out of this nightmare.

In my condition I wouldn't be able to sail the boat for much longer. Not unless my seasickness stopped and I was able to start eating again, but what were my options?

I pulled the waterproof chart up onto my lap and tried to get my brain to function.

Given my last estimated position and guestimating leeway. I reckoned that the gale had pushed us South Eastwards towards Ushant.

I thought that would now be about 40 miles away.

Ahead of me lay 350 miles of the Bay of Biscay to Spain, astern Falmouth 120 or so miles to windward.

Closing the French coast would be crazy.

It would mean crossing those busy shipping lanes off Ushant.

Not only that but the Westerly wind forecast would put me on a lee shore. And this was not just any lee shore. The Brittany coast has a fearsome reputation. Rocks, huge tides, fast currents and tricky harbour approaches to name but a few.

I didn't even have charts for the area.

Turning back would have meant at least 48 hours of hard beating. I wasn't physically capable of that and neither was 'Mor Gwas'. It was a non-starter. Even before considering the psychological effect of giving up.

It slowly dawned on me that there was only one option. To carry on.

We were where we were and that was that.

It's strange, but at the time the thought of getting outside help never even occurred to me. I had never carried a VHF radio on my boat so I had no means of summoning help from afar. I'd put myself into this situation, no one else was responsible and nor should they be. At that point in time, there was me the boat and the sea. I was going to have to cope on my own, simple as that.

Having made my decision, I felt better and concentrated on sailing the boat the best I could. The faster we sailed on the right course the sooner we'd be out of this mess.

I battled on all morning, trying to make progress. The wind was all over the place. Strong gusts that put the lee rail under and had me hanging onto the tiller. Calms that left the boat rolling around with the boom banging from side to side and the sail slatting.

Every movement I made was an effort and I'd stopped thinking clearly.

One time I looked at the compass and found I was steering 245 degrees instead of 215 degrees.

By lunchtime, the wind had got up again and I'd had to heave to once more.

I wasn't aware of it at the time but I realise now that I had reached my physical and mental limits. I didn't care what happened anymore.

Lethargy and resignation had slowly but surely pervaded body and mind.

Being alone deprived me of any chance that I'd snap out of it.

All it would have taken was a strong voice telling me to pull myself together, to get a grip and take command again.

This is where individual mental strength shows its hand, at the limits of endurance.

We all know stories of heroes and heroines who, in their hour of greatest challenge, managed to carry on. Managing to ignore the pain in their tortured bodies. Those with the mental strength to pick themselves up and keep going.

The survival training I'd received in the Navy had taught me that mental strength is the number one factor when the chips are down.

I feel somewhat ashamed now that I wasn't able to do that. I simply hadn't got that mental strength. I caved in and surrendered to the twin enemies of fatigue and fear. I just gave up.

Now I was shivering again but I seemed powerless to do anything about it.

I sat on the floor of the cockpit with glazed eyes, staring unfocused at the cold grey expanse of lumpy, white, foam topped water surrounding me.

I'd had enough and I desperately wanted it to stop.

That wasn't going to happen.

So my primitive brain exerted what little control it had and stopped me instead.

It suspended reality and shut my systems down, I was 54 hours out of Falmouth and I was close to finished.

I have no idea how long I stayed in the cockpit but at some point I guess my survival instinct kicked in. It decided that if I stayed there much longer I'd most likely die of hypothermia.

Somehow I mustered enough energy to crawl down into the cabin and collapse on my bunk, shivering and sick with fear.

16

Day 3 (Monday)

I MUST HAVE DRIFTED in and out of consciousness for most of the day.

It was late afternoon before something woke me from my stupor.

I pulled myself up to look out of the cabin window. The wind had picked up, the world outside was grey and hostile, I knew the storm was coming.

I felt totally numb, I no longer felt scared, I no longer felt lonely, I felt nothing at all.

As I started to slide back down onto my bunk I glanced out towards the stern once more. My heart nearly stopped.

I couldn't process what I was seeing, there, not a few hundred yards away was a sizeable fishing boat.

It's purposeful bluff bow shouldering the sea aside in heaps as it ploughed towards me.

I could even read the name on the bow, 'L'Zephir'.

I could see figures in yellow oilskins moving about on deck.

Suddenly I wasn't alone, suddenly the world I'd left behind had reappeared and I could see other humans.

It was unbelievable. It hadn't even crossed my mind that this could happen. With no VHF radio I was completely cut off and for days now my horizon had been empty.

I'd accepted the fact that it would probably stay that way for some time to come.

So to me, at that moment, this fishing boat may just as well have been an alien spacecraft. My amazement couldn't have been greater.

The boat was much closer now and I wasted no time in scrambling back into the cockpit. A surge of adrenaline shocked my body into the fastest movement it had managed in days.

I was waving and yelling even before I'd fully emerged from the cabin.

What these French fishermen must have made of the sight I can't imagine.

First they see a tiny little daysailer seemingly abandoned miles offshore.

Then an apparently demented apparition appears on deck, waving and yelling like a madman.

'L'Zephir' passed close astern of me, the crew lined up along the side shouting and pointing at me.

I just collapsed in the cockpit and cried, completely overwhelmed with the emotion of this human contact.

When I next looked up they were going away, I started to panic, my brain trying to understand, had they just been curious? Had they thought that 'Mor Gwas' was abandoned and that they could salvage her? Did they think my waving and shouting was just over excited 'bon ami'?

Whatever it was, I thought they were leaving me. I couldn't let that happen, I had to do something.

It took only seconds for me to realise what. I dived down below and grabbed the watertight container stowed next to the companionway. It contained my rescue flares. I frantically unscrewed the lid and pulled out a red hand flare.

Scrambling back into the cockpit I ripped off the plastic safety cover, held my arm out on the downwind side of the cockpit, and pulled the ignition cord.

I'd done this a few times before when I was in the Navy. I was ready for the sudden explosion of bright red light and gushing smoke that immediately sprouted from my clenched fist.

I looked away into the wind both to protect my eyes and to see where 'L'Zephir' was.

To my immense relief, I could see that she was turning slowly back towards me.

As the smoke and light from the flare died down I let it fall into the sea and once again sank back onto the cockpit floor.

I must have passed out again because I have no memory of the fishing boats final approach. The sudden burst of activity I'd put in when 'L'Zephir' appeared had drained the last dregs of energy from my body. My brain had decided that I need take no further part in the action other than to sit there and wait for salvation.

I have only a few memories of the actual rescue. It was dramatic, of that I'm sure.

Picture the scene.

The wind is blowing somewhere around 25 knots, there's a lumpy sea of perhaps 3 or 4 feet with swell probably twice that. Heaving about on this is an 18ft bilge keeled fibreglass daysailer with no sail up. In effect without command.

'L'Zephir' is a heavy displacement timber built Breton fishing boat in the region of 60ft long with a freeboard of 5 or 6ft.

As she comes alongside 'Mor Gwas' she's rolling heavily.

It was never going to be easy.

What I do remember is this.

As 'L'Zephir' came alongside, 'Mor Gwas' was repeatedly slammed into her thick timber sides. When the guys on board tried to grab the shrouds 'Mor Gwas' skewed inwards and her bowsprit snapped like a matchstick against the hull.

One of the fishermen tried jumping down into the cockpit but mistimed it and ended up in the water between the two boats.

Seeing one of my saviours in mortal danger must have jarred

me out of my stupor momentarily because I do remember trying to help.

God knows how he got out but he did. I have a vague memory of clutching a handful of thick wool sweater and oilskin jacket as I tried to help him into the cockpit.

My next memory is one of being manhandled over the bulwarks of 'L'Zephir' as the swell lifted 'Mor Gwas' within a few feet of the cappings.

Then, as 'Mor Gwas' dropped away again, of being pulled back away from them over the rail.

At some point before the boats came together, I'd clipped my safety harness onto the cockpit u-bolt. It was proof that my attempt to make this an automatic action when sailing alone had in fact been successful.

Now though this sensible precaution threatened to put me in serious danger. But with commendable efficiency one of the crew whipped out the knife attached to the bib of his oilskin trousers. It sliced through the line in an instant. As the line parted I fell hard onto the oily, wet deck and passed out again.

I came round down below in what seemed like a tropical fug of warmth.

Two guys were holding me up and stripping off my sodden clothes.

I was towelled down, put into some dry gear loaned from one of the crew and tucked into a bunk.

While this was happening the skipper of 'L'Zephir' was talking at me with what appeared to be some panic, repeating the words "Vous etes seul? Vous etes seul? I mustered enough brainpower to realise that he was asking if I was alone.

He was understandably concerned that there might have been someone with me who'd gone overboard.

I mumbled 'Oui Oui, Je suis seul, seul' then instantly fell asleep.

I have no idea how long I slept but I guess it was several hours. I was woken by one of the crew bearing a mug of strong black coffee which I sat up and gulped despite the scalding sensation in my throat.

I think I slept again after that and when I next woke I was helped up onto the bridge by one of the crew.

It was dark and 'L'Zephir' was now being thrown about by a sizeable sea. I looked out of the bridge windows and wondered how I would have survived the night on 'Mor Gwas'.

By way of broken French and sign language, I learned from the skipper that they had tried to take 'Mor Gwas' in tow. But that the sea conditions had made it impossible. She'd been cast adrift.

Amazingly, before they cut her loose, they'd somehow got back aboard and recovered my passport, wallet and watch.

When the skipper put these few salvaged belongings in my hands, I broke down.

It was all I could do to repeat the words "merci, merci" as my emotions got the better of me again.

As I was helped back to my bunk I just felt sick to my stomach.

'Mor Gwas' was gone. Everything I owned was gone. And through the numbness came the first feelings of shame and guilt. What had I done? What had I done?

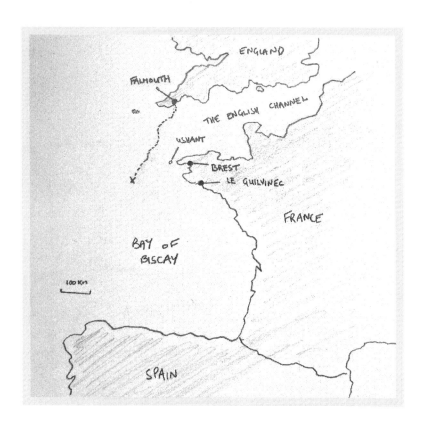

17

Le Guilvinec

L'ZEPHIR' steamed all night back towards her home port of Le
Guilvinec on the Brittany coast.

Unsurprisingly I slept for most of it.

I seem to remember being woken to eat hot soup and bread
with the crew at some point. Then, early in the morning, I was
taken back up to the bridge where, to my utter amazement, I got to
talk to my Dad on the radio telephone.

It was a short difficult emotional conversation.

He told me that one of my cousins had heard on the radio news
that a British yachtsman had been rescued in Biscay. Obviously my
folks had been frantic with worry the UK Coastguard had
arranged the call. It was good to be able to reassure them that I
was OK.

I stayed on the bridge for a while as we made our approach
into harbour past savage looking rocks rising out of breaking
waves.

It had been tough out at sea, but I thanked my stars that I'd not
been anywhere near this frightening coast.

Not long after, we tied up alongside the quay.

The place was busy with fishing vessels and vehicles and as I followed the skipper ashore I realised that a small crowd had gathered.

Murmured conversation and pointing were directed towards me. Obviously news of the rescue had already reached the harbour side.

As we reached the top of the stone steps a smart looking young lad in Naval Uniform came forward towards the skipper with arm outstretched. They shook hands and exchanged a few words and then he turned to me, again with hand outstretched, and greeted me in perfect English. "Good morning Monsieur Awk-Es-Ford, how are you? Are you OK? Do you need to go to the hospital"?

After thanking him and said I was just tired and that there was no need for a hospital. He asked if I was sure and I nodded again. "D'accord, well, in that case, I am to take you to Naval Headquarters in Brest, the Admiral wants to see you and there will be some paperwork to complete".

He took my arm and started to lead me through the crowd to a white car with Naval insignia on the door.

I stopped briefly and turned back to the skipper and crew of L'Zephir who by now were all lined up on the quayside. I waved and tried to shout "Merci beaucoup, Merci' beaucoup". I wished I had the language to say more but, to be honest, I'd have struggled, even in English.

The drive to Brest took about an hour. The young sub-lieutenant, Eric, was friendly and sympathetic as he asked me how I came to be at sea in such a small boat.

I gave him the gist of my story and he seemed impressed. But I was soon to experience an entirely different reaction.

As we arrived at Naval HQ the sentry opened the big steel gates and saluted as we pulled into a cobbled courtyard. After checking in at the security desk, I was given a visitors pass and then followed Eric down the wide highly decorated corridors.

I felt distinctly out of place. I hadn't washed since leaving Falmouth. I was wearing my yellow wellies, a salt-encrusted pair of jeans with ripped knee, my sailing jacket and a tee shirt.

I was thirsty and the building seemed boiling hot, my head swam.

We stopped outside a huge pair of ornately carved wooden doors alongside which sat a female naval officer behind a large desk. Eric said a few words in French and nodded his head towards me. She acknowledged and pressed a button on her intercom. A sharp voice answered and she indicated to Eric we should go through. He removed his hat, ran his fingers through his hair, jammed the hat under his arm and stiffened up. I guessed we were about to meet the Admiral.

As Eric marched smartly into the grand office I followed on behind and then stopped alongside him in front of yet another huge wooden desk.

Behind it sat the Admiral. His face was stony and he looked at me as if I was something he'd stepped in on the pavement, completely ignoring Eric as he saluted.

For the next fifteen minutes or so I was interrogated. There's no other word for it. If the Admiral spoke any English he wasn't going to use it and Eric had to act as interpreter.

I was threatened with arrest for the crime of abandoning my boat in French Territorial waters and endangering shipping. I was quizzed left right and centre about why I was at sea in such a small boat. Why I'd set off a flare. What qualifications I had. Why I was endangering other vessels and their crews. I was treated with utter contempt and made to feel like a criminal and it was all too much.

I was already mentally shattered and dead on my feet. I did my best to answer the questions truthfully and politely but eventually I just hung my head and mumbled incoherently.

The Admiral lost patience and dismissed us gruffly, I felt sorry for Eric, I may have deserved such treatment, but he'd done nothing to receive it.

On our way out Eric apologised and tried to explain that this particular guy had a bad reputation at the best of times. I didn't care. Nothing mattered to me just then. I was beginning to feel like it might have been better if I'd just slipped silently beneath the waves out there.

Eric could plainly see that I was finished. On the way back to Le Guilvinec we stopped at his rented apartment and he knocked up a quick lunch. Bread, cold meats and cheese washed down with some vin rouge. I'd eaten nothing since the soup on board 'L'Zephir' so it was a delight.

Eric asked me more about my life and sailing. Once again I got the feeling that, in complete contrast to L'Admiral, he actually admired my adventurous spirit.

Thanks to the wine I slept for the rest of the journey back to Le Guilvinec.

I woke as we pulled up outside a small hotel on the opposite side of the quay from where we'd landed. Eric spoke to the receptionist and a room key was handed over. He gave it to me and pointed up the stairs. "You have a room on the second floor" he said, "I'll be back at 9 in the morning to pick you up, sleep well my friend".

I nodded and plodded up the stairs to find a tiny room basically furnished. I gulped some water from the tap, stripped off my filthy clothes and got between the sheets. I didn't know what time it was. I didn't know what was going to happen next. I just knew that I was safe and for tonight at least I could sleep peacefully.

The next thing I heard was a loud knocking at the door. It was 9 am and Eric was back, I'd slept for 18 hours. I answered the door in my underpants and once he realised I'd just woken he told me to take a shower and meet him downstairs for breakfast.

I still felt out of it, my mind raced to try and take in where I was and what had happened. The hot shower helped but I still had only the clothes I stood up in and once again felt very self-conscious as I walked into the restaurant to find Eric.

The table was loaded with croissants and toast, coffee and conserves. I was ravenous again and tucked in enthusiastically. Eric asked if I felt better then said he had some news.

Apparently when 'L'Zephir' had abandoned 'Mor Gwas' they'd reported her last known position to the French Coastguard. The following day the French Navy had sent out some sort of salvage vessel and they'd found 'Mor Gwas' adrift. She'd been craned up onto the deck and would be back in Brest by now.

I couldn't believe it, my faithful little boat had survived, my home, everything I owned, I was going to get them back.

Eric jolted me back to reality.

It wasn't going to be that simple. He told me that I wouldn't be allowed to see her until the full salvage amount had been paid and that it was likely to be in the region of £5000. I was shattered, there was no way I could pay that amount, nor anything close. 'Mor Gwas' represented my sole worth and the boat and everything on her weren't worth half that. He understood, but explained this was not something he had any power to change.

I knew now that there was nothing left for me to do here in France. All I could do was get back to England and try to earn enough money to pay the fee, it was my only option.

I told Eric what I was thinking and asked if he could get me back to Brest where I could sort out a ferry ticket. He nodded and said it should be OK but that I couldn't leave France without permission from the Navy. He didn't think it would be a problem, they knew I could do nothing here.

By now I was getting sick of walking around looking like a tramp. I asked if I could at least get aboard 'Mor Gwas' to pick up clean clothes, some toiletries and a few personal possessions for the journey.

He shook his head. 'Mor Gwas' was no longer mine. She, and everything aboard her now belonged to the French Navy and The Admiral wouldn't permit it. I put my head in my hands and found my eyes watering again, this was all too much and I just couldn't cope.

Eric suggested I stay at the hotel for the morning as he had other business to attend to but that he'd come back at lunchtime.

I went back to my room and lay on the bed for a while, my

head reeling. I thought I might sleep again, but I couldn't. So I got up and went for a walk around the harbour just to get some air in my lungs. I walked slowly, half lost in my thoughts and half taking in the sights and sounds of a busy French fishing harbour.

Suddenly a big hand slapped down on my shoulder making me jump and I heard "Nee el, l'anglaise, ca va!"

I turned to see a couple of guys I immediately recognised as crew of 'L'Zephir' and they all but dragged me into the nearby bar. I protested, I felt bad. I still had no money and if there was anyone in the world I should be buying drinks for it was these guys. But they insisted, and soon we were sitting around a table with a large jug of Pastis.

It was surreal, I tried to pick up on the conversation but failed miserably. So I just sat there nodding and smiling occasionally. It seemed that they just wanted to show me off to the other fishermen in the bar. I could tell from the dramatic hand gestures that they were telling the story of my rescue in great detail.

I lost track of time and the alcohol was starting to take effect. Next thing I knew Eric was standing alongside me with a big grin on his face. He chatted with my rescuers for a few minutes then we said our goodbyes. Outside he said, "Neil we're going to see your boat, when we get there you can go onboard for 5 minutes, no longer. I have arranged it but please respect the time or I will be in big trouble".

I was elated. On our drive to Brest he seemed a little quiet, I told him that grateful though I was, I didn't want him to risk some sort of disciplinary issue for my sakes. He assured me it was OK. He'd arranged things with the yardmaster and the Admiral was out of town, it'd be OK.

We pulled into the dockyard and drove past lots of buildings and sheds before pulling up outside one that looked like a giant Nissen hut. It was a semi-circular construction made of corrugated iron. As we entered through a side door I realised it was a boathouse and it was full of sailing dinghies and rowboats.

I didn't see 'Mor Gwas' until we were almost on top of her. The mast was down on the deck and she looked a sorry state. Her appearance wasn't helped by the gloomy yellow light cast from dusty old lamps high up in the eaves of the shed.

Eric was looking around all the time as if expecting to be caught and I began to doubt if he'd actually got any sort of permission to be here.

"Quickly Neil, please," he said. I jumped into the cockpit and lifted the washboard. The cabin sole was awash, everything was wet. I tried to control my emotions and concentrate on the task at hand.

I found a kit bag, lifted the bunk cushion and retrieved a bag full of clothes that I'd sealed in a plastic sack. I grabbed a pair of deck shoes, what else? I couldn't think. Eric hissed again "Neil we must go" I looked around feverishly for my big sailing knife, it had gone, as had my camera. I grabbed my small brass barometer off the bulkhead, my log books and then remembered my wash bag and a towel. Eric was now hissing again obviously stressed.

I climbed out of the cabin quickly. Put the washboard back in place and just managed a last glance back at my beloved boat before we were out into the bright sunshine and away.

I was gutted, I'd abandoned my boat again, and I was once more being made to feel like a criminal. I felt myself losing control again but managed to hold things together.

Once outside the gate Eric seemed to relax, his relief was obvious and I thanked him once again.

He then told me that permission had been given for me to return to England and that he'd checked and there was a ferry leaving from Roscoff that evening. If I wanted he could drive me to the ticket office and then later to Roscoff to catch the boat.

I didn't need to think about the answer. After we'd got the ticket Eric took me back to his apartment where I took a long shower and was able to put on clean clothes for the first time in 5 days. When you've lost everything small things like that feel amazing.

I felt a lot better despite my sense of shame and loss, now I had to regroup somehow and find a way to get my boat back.

It's a mark of how much 'Mor Gwas' had become part of me that as I boarded the ferry that night I didn't really think of it as going home. I was leaving my home behind stuck in a dingy shed in a dirty dockyard in Brest and I wouldn't be happy until I got her back.

I'll be forever grateful to Eric, his kindness to me during those difficult 48 hours saved me from a complete breakdown. He stuck his neck out for me and I wish I'd been able to show my appreciation with more than a few words.

I very much hope that he is now an Admiral.

18

Picking Up The Pieces

IT TOOK most of June and July that year to sort out the salvage.

They were a stressful few months as I lived in limbo, wondering if I'd ever see 'Mor Gwas' again. I kept getting letters from the French Navy demanding immediate payment or my boat would be 'disposed of'. Communication was time-consuming and difficult. When they discovered that 'Mor Gwas' wasn't insured things turned into a bit of a farce.

It may seem strange to some that I had no insurance. But it would have been nigh on impossible to get any sort of cover for the trip I'd planned even if I'd been able to afford it. The salvage 'system' couldn't cope with that. They had expected that their claim would simply be settled by an insurance company.

Not having one to deal with really threw a spanner in the works. They stuck to their demands. I had no choice but stick to mine. I quite genuinely couldn't pay what they were asking.

Time dragged on.

Negotiations were helped enormously by one of my father's business acquaintances in France. Dad's Company did a lot of business with a French flooring manufacturer and the MD there took a great interest in helping me out. We never really found out what happened, but eventually he managed to get the entire salvage fee waived.

Even better he got confirmation that for a nominal charge of £ 130 to cover 'storage' 'Mor Gwas' would be released back to me.

I was over the moon, and late in July I packed a bag and once more headed across the Channel.

The months ashore had restored me physically and I'd had plenty of time to think about what had happened.

Many expressed surprise that I was now eager to return to the life I'd had before.

They figured that my experience would have put me off the sea and sailing for life. That I'd now settle down to a 'normal' life.

It had crossed my mind I'll admit. I'd had a very close shave and all but lost everything, that was true. But I began to see that although I'd been through hell, the time I'd had on 'Mor Gwas' before that had given me some of the most incredible experiences of my life. I'd been happier and healthier than I could ever remember. I'd learned a hard lesson for sure, but I'd survived and I was stronger for it. I needed to get back to that life.

I'd been told to report to the Navy Club Nautique in Brest when I arrived. I got there about 11.30 am already tired after a long train/ ferry/ train trip.

At the reception desk I introduced myself and asked for the Manager. I think he must have been related to my old nemesis L'Admiral. He certainly had the same attitude of disdain towards me. All politeness was discarded as he immediately asked if I had the necessary payment.

I succeeded in annoying him even more when I explained that I still only had Sterling in my pocket. So he got his equally disdainful wife to drive me to the nearest bank to get it exchanged.

After he had the equivalent of £ 130 in his pocket he took me down to the quayside and got a boatman to run me out to 'Mor Gwas'. She'd been moved out of the boathouse and I spotted her bobbing about on a mooring some distance off the quay.

She looked worse than I remembered.

The last time I'd seen her I'd just had a few minutes. The light had been poor and she'd been surrounded by other boats. Now, out here in the sunlight, her condition was plain to see.

Her bowsprit broken and hanging off the bow.

The mast was lying on deck with weed covered shrouds dangling in the water. Broken guard rail stanchions. Several holes in the deck where cleats had been ripped out. Bent mast tabernacle. Dodgers hanging loose. Big black scuff marks down her hull. She'd obviously been providing a comfortable roosting platform for the seagulls as well. She looked a total wreck.

The boatman put me aboard and then using hand signals seemed to be offering to help me get the mast up. I think he thought I was just going to sail away. I politely declined, and he shrugged his shoulders and motored away.

I dumped my bag in the cockpit noticing as I did so the gaping hole in the coaming where the port sheet winch had once been. With heart sinking, I lifted the hatch and washboard. The cabin was a disaster, ruined books and charts scattered about. Water over the cabin sole. A horrible smell of damp and what I suspected was rotting food.

I'd recovered physically but, truth be told, I was still weak mentally. Tears welled up in my eyes as I surveyed this little space that had been my home for so long.

Once again I felt ashamed that I'd let my noble little boat down, that I'd let her suffer like this.

There was only one thing to do and that was to get cracking with sorting things out.

I pumped the bilges dry. Ditched about 25 rusted cans of food and a big bag of sodden rice over the side. Then started working my way through my possessions saving what I could.

I noticed that my sheath knife, seaman's knife, big torch and a set of keys were missing. I felt angry at first, it was like my house had been burgled.

But then I remembered that I had in fact relinquished all claim to 'Mor Gwas' when I'd been pulled onto the deck of 'L'Zephir'.

From that point on all that was mine became free to whomsoever found it next, It was my own fault.

After a couple of hours the boatman returned. Using sign language and my lousy French I established that he was offering to tow me over to a pontoon berth. It'd give me room to spread my gear out and work on 'Mor Gwas' more easily. I readily accepted.

I spent the rest of the afternoon there in the pleasant sunshine. I threw myself into the work, shutting out all negative thoughts. Totally focused on making 'Mor Gwas' habitable again.

In the early evening about 6 pm, the friendly boatman returned. He told me that I needed to pack up now and that I wasn't allowed to stay onboard overnight.

I nearly lost it. I had gear all over the pontoon. I'd had virtually nothing to eat all day. I was hot and tired and now I faced the prospect of roaming the streets looking for a hotel. I think my mood came over and he disappeared for 15 minutes or so. When he returned I gathered that he was offering to tow 'Mor Gwas' round to the nearby harbour 'Basin'. There I could moor for free and stay on board as long as I liked.

We threw all my gear back aboard 'Mor Gwas', tied his launch alongside and he motored us the short distance round to the small stone inner harbour.

I tied up alongside a couple of neglected fishing boats. The water was dirty. Diesel and rubbish floated around on the surface. There was a strong smell of fish and fuel in the air. The town lay just behind the wall, traffic and car horns made a cacophony of sound. It was hot and humid and I was shattered.

I found a salvageable tin of beef stew and heated it up on the Primus but despite my hunger I had to force it down.

The day had taken its toll. I'd been working on autopilot, trying not to think too much. But I'd seen enough of 'Mor Gwas' to know that she needed some pretty extensive and expensive repairs. Apart from the broken bowsprit, cut rigging and ripped rubbing strakes, the mast tabernacle was severely bent. One of the sheet winches was missing.

Also I'd seen a nasty looking crack in the gel coat running a good distance along the hull midships on the starboard side. The interior hull lining stopped me establishing if it was visible inside the boat, but it looked bad. I suspected that the hull might well have suffered some serious crushing at some point.

My plan had been simple. Get back to 'Mor Gwas', sort her out, do what I needed to do to get her sailing again and then to sail her back to Falmouth and start again. In Falmouth I'd be able to restore her to her former glory, I could pick up where I'd left off, work for Clive again, make new plans. But now as I sat in the wrecked cabin of an unseaworthy boat in the filthy hot basin of a foreign port I realised that just wasn't possible.

I had neither the money nor the wherewithal to make that happen and I began to think that this could be the end of my adventures aboard 'Mor Gwas'.

But I wasn't ready to accept it yet, I couldn't give up that easily. I collapsed into my bunk and slept. My first night aboard since abandoning her off Ushant nearly two months before.

I woke the following morning after a very restless nights sleep in oppressive heat to find my arms covered in mosquito bites. The sun was shining though and I felt a bit better. So once more I threw myself into work trying to get 'Mor Gwas' looking like a boat again.

I removed the broken bowsprit and stanchions and patched the holes in the deck. I even managed to straighten the tabernacle and get the mast raised with temporary rigging. I washed everything down and to be fair by the end of the day 'Mor Gwas' looked a lot better.

She looked like someone owned her at least, but it was an illusion and I knew it.

The killer blow had come that afternoon when I peeled back the carpet cabin lining behind the gel coat crack I'd spotted on the outside of the hull. I could see straight away that some serious damage had been done. Strands of glass fibre stuck out of the crack

143

and I could see sunlight shining through the hull, in places my fingers were able to flex the hullside.

I'd taken a closer look at the other side of the boat as well and although not as bad there were signs of stress there also. I remembered only too well the pounding she'd taken up against the solid wooden hull of L'Zephir. God knows what else she'd been put through when the Navy recovered her.

All I knew was that this was evidence of serious structural damage way beyond my abilities to repair. There was no way I could sail across the Channel with the boat in this condition.

It must have been about 6 pm when I lay down on my bunk feeling completely shattered. I was hot and drenched in sweat, the mosquito bites on my arms had swelled red and raw from constant itching. I had a pounding headache. Once again everything piled in on me and this time I broke down.

I buried my face in the pillow to stifle my sobs, I felt completely and utterly ashamed lost and alone. I'd failed 'Mor Gwas' before and now I was going to fail her again.

It was obvious to me now that there was only one thing left to do.

I had to try and sell 'Mor Gwas' as she stood for whatever I could get for her, carry as much away as I could and go back to England.

It broke my heart.

I must have eaten something and slept somehow. But all I recall is that the following morning I was woken early by activity on one of the fishing boats I was tied too.

Sticking my head out of the companionway I was greeted with a jovial grin and a 'Bonjour' from a guy whom I presumed to be the owner.

He spoke no English but as my poor French was beginning to return we were able to strike up a semblance of conversation.

He introduced himself as Vincent. He could see that my boat had been damaged and no doubt guessed I'd been through the mill a bit as well.

He asked if I was sailing back to England, I said it wasn't possible, that the boat needed too much work and that I must sell her.

He understood and seemed to be saying that he knew someone who might be interested. He said that he'd return the following morning and drive me down the road to the marina at Port Pleasance where I could meet someone. With that, he waved goodbye and motored out of the harbour.

There wasn't a lot I could do onboard and I needed a break, so I decided to walk into town. It wasn't far and I tried to forget my problems as I did the tourist thing walking about and taking in the sights.

In anticipation of leaving I bought a wheeled suitcase because I knew I wouldn't be able to carry everything I wanted to take off 'Mor Gwas'.

I ate a simple meal in town that evening washed down with a few beers. I still felt very lost, very lonely and very sad, but I'd made my decision and that at least gave me some comfort.

I slept a bit better and was up early the following morning to wait for my fisherman friend. It was a long couple of hours. For most of the time I convinced myself that either I'd misunderstood or he wasn't going to show.

Then about mid-morning, a battered 2CV van pulled up on the quay and sounded it's horn and I recognised my fisherman. I clambered over the rafted up boats alongside 'Mor Gwas', up the rusty quay ladder, and into the van.

It was a short drive to the marina and as we pulled up outside the office I saw that we were going into a little broker's office based in a portacabin.

From the photos in the window, he obviously specialised in small craft, which looked promising.

Vincent introduced me to a smart chap by the name of Monsieur Trouville who thankfully spoke good English.

I explained that I needed to sell my boat and gave him a brief description. He knew of the Silhouette and said that he could probably sell her for me. His commission was 10% and he thought he'd have no problem selling within a few weeks.

I couldn't hide my disappointment and there seemed little point in trying to be smart. I was in no position to haggle, I'd already said I needed to sell and now I told him I needed to sell quickly and for cash. I could tell he saw an opportunity to make more money out of the deal but good businessman that he was, he played it cool.

"Peut etre" he said, "perhaps I might be interested. I'll come and see the boat this afternoon".

He exchanged a few words with Vincent. No doubt to explain what he could expect to get out of the deal, and then Vincent drove me back to the boat.

I stayed onboard all afternoon waiting for Monsieur Trouville, once again wondering if he'd show.

He finally arrived just after four.

He came aboard and looked around giving nothing away.

Despite the work I'd done, I knew 'Mor Gwas' still looked bad. I told him that I was taking the wind generator, the Walker log and my personal possessions but that everything else came with the boat. The outboard, the dinghy, self-steering the lot.

He thought for a few minutes then offered FF5000 which was the equivalent of about £ 1600. It didn't seem a lot and I tried to push him up, but he knew I was desperate.

He was buying as seen and I almost told him about the hull damage, but he knew boats, he could see what I could see. In any case with all the other gear aboard, he wasn't going to lose out.

I'd paid £ 1200 for 'Mor Gwas' nearly two years before, I was losing out in more ways than one, but I was in no position to bargain.

We shook hands and he said he'd return at 9: 30 the following morning with the cash.

That evening I dismounted the LVM and packed as much as I possibly could into my old Navy kitbag and the new wheeled case I'd bought.

I slept badly, half praying that he'd show up the next day and that this would be my last night aboard 'Mor Gwas' and half wishing that it wouldn't be. I was in a bad way.

True to his word though Monsieur Trouville appeared next morning as promised and handed over the cash.

He helped me get my kit ashore and offered to drive me to the station.

I declined, it was a stupid thing to do. I had to walk nearly a mile with stuff I could barely carry.

But I needed to walk, I needed to be on my own.

I didn't even look back at my once beautiful boat and in any case I'd have struggled to see her through the tears.

This really was the end of my foolish voyage.

19

Still Foolish

IN THE MONTHS that followed I gradually came to terms with
what had happened.

I could so easily have lost my life, I'd tested myself and failed.

I'd set out trying to emulate in some way what Shane Acton
had done aboard 'Shrimpy'. I'd chosen my boat well, I'd prepared
her well and, I thought, I'd prepared myself well. For all that there
was no avoiding the harsh reality - I hadn't been up to the
challenge.

And the more I thought about it the more I felt like a failure.

Although nothing was ever said to my face I knew what people
were thinking. Many of my friends and family thought that I'd got
no more than I deserved for my stupidity. How could there
possibly have been any other outcome?

I'd been stupid enough to set out to sail the ocean in a daysailer. It was bound to end badly wasn't it?

They couldn't be blamed. They didn't know any different. But I
did. And I knew that others with experience of the sea knew it too,
not least Clive.

'Mor Gwas' had been up to the trip but I hadn't. It was as
simple as that.

I'd abandoned a boat that was perfectly seaworthy. Even after I'd left her she survived, bobbing about quite happily. Despite being so badly treated bashing up against 'L'Zephir'. Even after being abused during the recovery, she'd come out more or less in one piece.

I knew in my heart that I'd made the right decision to sell her. But I also carried the guilt of having abandoned her yet again, despite being given a second chance.

I guess all of this sounds a bit crazy. I've been talking about that collection of fibreglass wood and metal as if it were a person. But as all sailors know, ships and boats do that to you.

For months I was lost. Even if I'd had the funds to buy another boat I wouldn't have been able to do it. I'd been damaged and it would take me a long time to heal. Despite all that, my yearning for the sea never left me.

If I'd known how long it would take me to get back to sailing I'd perhaps have done things differently. Understandably those around me pretty much assumed that I was finished with the whole thing. After what I'd been through there was no way I'd want to sail again was there? It was easy to go along. Nothing said, just assumptions. They thought one thing I thought another. Sometimes doubting myself, other times knowing that one day I'd have to return.

I started working for my father in the flooring industry. It was a career path I'd set out to avoid but now it was an obvious choice. Not easy, just obvious. Making that choice trapped me for 20 years.

I met a girl, we married, we had a beautiful daughter. We lost the house in the property crash of the late 80' s when interest rates went up to 15%. The banks had been throwing money at us. I had a huge mortgage, credit cards were maxed out, it had to end in tears and it did. Our marriage broke up. I lost everything, again. Looking back I don't know why I didn't return to the sea when that happened. But I didn't, I picked myself up and got back on the treadmill.

A few years later I was in another relationship. Back with a mortgage and throwing myself into renovating an old house.

I worked like a dog. My job took me around the country, driving 1000 miles a week. High-pressure site meetings. Evenings and weekend spent on DIY late into the night. It was madness and guess what? My life fell apart yet again.

Yet again I lost everything and found myself alone in a rented apartment. This time I struggled to keep going, I hadn't seen it coming, I was heartbroken. It felt like my life was over.

During the previous years when times got tough, I often thought of escape. It's an overused phrase but one that was often on my lips 'there must be more to life than this'. And yet I carried on doing what everyone else was doing, getting nowhere fast. When my thoughts turned to the sea I thought about doing things differently. Not just sailing for sailing's sake but living a lifestyle that fitted with the sea. A lifestyle that was the polar opposite of the whirlwind life I was leading.

I'd never forgotten Tim and Heather's big catamaran 'Ika Roa' and the similar boat 'Imagine' owned by Steve Turner. I remembered vividly the first time I'd seen them back on Church Beach in Penryn. How impressed I'd been by these simple strong sailing machines. I did a bit of research and established that they were the designs of a guy by the name of James Wharram. He lived down in Cornwall and three times in 20 years I sent off for his brochure and spent hours going through it.

His design book was like nothing I'd ever seen before. I'd been expecting a technical manual of some sort detailing all the boats and their attributes. To some degree, that's what it was. But rather than technical drawings the book contained beautiful pencil sketches of the boats. Sometimes at sea, and often with naked girls lounging on the deck. The more I read the more I felt in tune with the philosophy they talked about.

Sea People, living cheaply and simply, cruising the world's oceans.

It took a long long time for the seed to germinate but it was first planted back in those dark days of craziness.

Yet for all the dreaming it took an eternity for me to realise that dreaming wasn't going to get me where I longed to be. That I'd actually have to get off my arse and do something.

The years of conditioning, peer pressure and social constraints had a far stronger level of control that I realised. Despite the almost constant feelings of discontent and longing for change, the bonds of normality held fast. They locked me into a cycle in which I simply repeated past mistakes.

There's a quote that says:

'If you keep doing what you've always done you'll keep getting what you've always got'

That's exactly what I was doing. My two partners during these times showed no interest in my occasional dabbling with dreams of giving it all up and sailing away. They were well and truly into normality, a good job, a nice home, a nice car, shopping as a leisure activity and a couple of decent holidays a year. That was all they needed.

This normality came with a toxic side effect though. it's something that society, in general, seems to miss. I'm talking about the concept of 'enough'. It's become the norm hasn't it? We all desire more. More money, more stuff, more everything. And yet there's never a point at which we say 'brilliant I've done it, I've got what I've always wanted, I have enough, I can be happy now'. Because when we get that thing, when we reach that point, we don't even take the time to appreciate it. Without even pausing to draw breath we immediately move our attention to something else. A bigger house, a smarter car, a more exotic holiday. I called it toxic and that's what it is, because it kills any chance of happiness and leaves us in a constant state of want. It leaves us unable to appreciate the here and now, unable to appreciate what we have. In the words of Mick Jagger:

'I can't get no satisfaction'

It took me half a century of living before my eyes were opened to the madness of it all.

Half a century before I found myself so depressed that I spent entire weekends in bed. Entire nights scrolling through channel after channel of crap on the TV. Entire days where I did nothing except wish that I was dead. Thinking that I'd made such a mess of my life that the only hope was to end it and see if I got another one.

Perhaps that's what it takes. Perhaps a person needs to find themselves at that point where all the things we are brought up to believe are important become meaningless. Where it seems like there really is nothing to lose.

I don't know, I don't have the intelligence or intellect to give advice. All I can do is tell you what happened to me, how I came to this watershed in my life, how I was able to change.

Maybe it will resonate with others, maybe it will help, I hope so.

All I know for sure is that it could have gone either way. It's entirely possible that my days may have ended back then.

But there was still a tiny flame somewhere deep down that had never died. It was a flame that 'Mor Gwas' had sparked. It was a flame that had burnt brightly for a few years before being all but extinguished by the cold waters of Biscay. Now, as I found myself lost and seemingly without hope, the coldness within me revealed its continued presence.

Feeble though it was it shone like a long searched for harbour light on a dark and stormy night. It gave me something to focus on, it gave me hope and I started moving towards it.

After months of stagnation, months of near drowning in the polluted waters of bad memories, this little flame saved me. I struck out for it and as I drew nearer it warmed me more and more. Hope returned followed soon after by enthusiasm.

I dug out my old ragged copy of the Wharram design book.

Once more I spent hours reading and re-reading it but this time it was different. This time I wasn't just dreaming, this time I was determined to take action.

Not long after, I narrowed down my choice of design and sent off for study plans, a Tiki 31, a Tiki 38, a Tiki 46. These were Polynesian catamarans, capable of crossing oceans, boats that could provide a home. Even better they were boats that could be built comparatively cheaply by anyone with basic DIY skills and tools.

I no longer wasted my time with mindless TV. I read, I poured over the plans, I researched, I made notes, I dreamt.

I made a decision. A life-changing decision. I would build a Wharram Tiki 38 catamaran, I'd make her my home and I'd live the life I knew I was meant to live but that I'd suppressed for so long.

I was alive again.

Appendix

'Gleda' sailed out of Falmouth marina in April 2015.

From our berth there I could see Church Beach.

Before we left I walked around to where 'Mor Gwas' used to sit.

There's a new concrete walkway along the beach now, but

apart from that it's still the same. The trees I tied the bow lines to, even bits of my rock causeway sticking out of the slime.

Thousands of tides have long since washed away the impression of her keels from the mud, but they can't wash away memories.

Fixed above the navigation table aboard 'Gleda' is the wooden hand carved nameplate I unscrewed from the washboard on my last day aboard 'Mor Gwas'. I'm looking at it now as I write these final words and I'm smiling. It took thirty years, but 'Mor Gwas' finally crossed Biscay and made it to Portugal and the Mediterranean.

She's not finished yet.

Maybe my foolish voyage wasn't so foolish after all.

Thank You

So all that remains is to say a big "thank you" for buying and reading my book. I hope you enjoyed it.

I know you'll have seen this same request in many other books you've read, but I'm going to ask just the same. Could you please take a minute or two to leave a review? It's really important for me to hear what you thought about it. Good or bad I want to know. I'm striving to improve my writing and your feedback will help me do that. Thanks.

Alternatively you can email me *neil@neilhawkesford.com*

DON'T FORGET YOUR FREE BOOK!
Visit https://www.neilhawkesford.com

Acknowledgments

Writing your first book is a challenge. Putting it out into the world for others to see is a greater one. When your words describe deep personal experience and emotion it's terrifying. My sincere thanks go to all the beta-readers who read that shoddy first edit.

In particular I'd like to thank those that contributed with comments and corrections.

You gave me the courage to publish.

- Craig Anderson
- Dody Tonga
- Ifor Davies
- Jackie Byrne
- John Harris
- Michael Stephani
- Michael West
- Peter Brook
- Rob Hughes
- Stuart McCullough
- Zvika Shalgo

My good friend **Jon Kutassy** deserves special mention. He spent hours proof-reading for me and is a long-time supporter of my foolishness. Thank you Jon.

For this second edition my particular thanks go to **Andrew Mar**. His emailed list of errors/corrections was extremely helpful.

Also by Neil Hawkesford

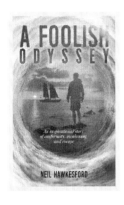

The foolishness continues..

Thirty years after losing 'Mor Gwas' I finally made it back to the sea.

A Foolish Odyssey is the sequel to this book. It's far longer and it was far harder to write. It's subtitle is;

An inspirational story of conformity, awakening and escape

I do hope you'll read it.

The book is available on Amazon.

Made in the USA
Columbia, SC
04 December 2019

84379305R00105